# Mindful Chef

Healthy You, Happy Planet

MYLES HOPPER & GILES HUMPHRIES

# *Mindful Chef*

## Healthy You, Happy Planet

CENTURY

The UN Environment Programme estimates that roughly one third of all food produced in the world is either lost or wasted and a vast amount of that waste is generated through traditional supply chains and within people's homes. With a recipe box, you can reduce your food waste by 21% compared to a supermarket shop. That's a powerful impact when multiplied across millions of meals. When you add to that our unique high welfare sourcing standards and obsessive focus on provenance, or the way we create recipes that align with the Planetary Health Diet guidelines (see page 22), that impact becomes even more pronounced. Eating the Mindful Chef way really can help customers have a better, more positive impact on our planet.

The name 'Mindful' encapsulates all that we intended to be as a company: to use our business as a real force for good and change.

Never before has this been more important. The world is experiencing a global climate emergency and food will play an integral role in helping us to mitigate some of the unintended consequences we now face as a society, largely as a result of the decisions we've made and our collective impact on the planet. But by making small changes to our daily and weekly routines, collectively we really can have a positive impact on the planet's future. That has always been one of our core beliefs as a business – that as a community we are able to create lasting change.

So why this book and why now? We are so proud of our first book *Eat Well, Live Better*, which we wrote in 2017 when we were still running our business from our little apartment in southwest London. There were fewer than 10 of us back then, so being asked by one of the world's biggest publishers to write a book about our mission and journey was a dream come true. Since then our team has grown to over 100 amazing people and we deliver tens of thousands of recipe boxes as well as prepared meals and smoothies, breakfasts and snacks all over the country every single week! We are proud as punch to be in the top 3% of B Corp food companies in the world (for more on what that means see page 28) thanks to our focus on the environment and using our community as a positive force for change. Probably most importantly, however, we've also donated over 16 million school meals to children living in poverty through our charity partner One Feeds Two. We operate a 'one for one' charity model, which means that for every meal we sell, we donate a school meal to a child.

We really believe there is something very special about Mindful Chef and our community but we know there are always things we can improve on. When you are producing 40 different recipes every week that need to be varied, have to constantly delight and excite customers to keep them interested it is nearly impossible for all those ingredients to be both local and hyper seasonal. That is the brilliance of this book. To create these recipes we were able to draw solely from local and seasonal produce – delicious and interesting ingredients of which our island nation has an abundance. Our hope is that you will use this book on evenings when you don't have a recipe box or when you have had the time to visit your local farmers' market or greengrocer and need inspiration for how to use the seasonal ingredients you have purchased.

But beyond the recipes, this book is also a fantastic opportunity to share everything we've learned as a company about food production and its impact on the world around us. In doing so we'll hopefully inspire you to be more aware of your own choices and how you might change the ways you shop and cook, so that not only are they better for you but for the planet too.

# The Mindful Chef Approach

When we started delivering boxes to our first customers' homes in 2015 we had what we believed was a fairly simple approach to nutrition and our recipes. We believed (and still do) that many people get caught up in the latest diets, fads and over-analyse what is already an extremely complicated and personal area – nutrition. Before starting Mindful Chef we were also guilty of this. Living in London we both worked long hours, returning home often late in the evenings, too tired to pull together a really healthy tasty dinner. Having grown up in the West Country, being used to home-cooked meals and spending any of our spare time outdoors or playing sport we knew there had to be a better way of giving our bodies what they needed rather than just settling for less nutritious, boring dinners.

So Mindful Chef was created. We decided to take it back to the basics and create food that's good for you, delicious and quick. You can expect to come away from every Mindful Chef meal feeling satisfied yet energised. There's no fasting or crash-dieting, you'll find yourselves eating lots of nutritious vegetables and flavoursome natural produce. We believe in eating less but higher-quality meat and fish, increasing the amount of vegetables on plates and reducing the amount of gluten and dairy in our weekly dinners. In fact, we don't include gluten or dairy in our recipes. That isn't to say we are gluten-free or dairy-free warriors. Far from it, we enjoy our pizzas and ice cream, however the reality is that most of us eat too many of these types of foods at the expense of including enough vegetables in our diet. We also wanted our recipes to be eaten by as many people as possible, so by leaving out a few ingredients (foods that might contain gluten or dairy) we can allow more people to experience the delicious, healthy meals we send out every week, including those who might not normally be able to due to allergies or intolerances.

Of course we also have more in-depth science-based nutritional criteria based on macro and micronutrients, overall calorie numbers and ensuring an inverse ratio of fats to carbohydrates which we apply to all of our recipes, including those in this book. For most of us this level of information is too much to take on board and doesn't necessarily help create a healthy, meaningful relationship with food. By allowing us to take care of the nutritional side of things you are able to enjoy these recipes knowing that they will be healthy, varied, good for you and tasty. Cooking up Mindful Chef recipes on a regular basis has visible health benefits. Our customers have reported feeling leaner, being more productive, having more focus and generally feeling healthier. There's nothing groundbreaking in this book, nor are there any quick fixes. We believe in balance and that food is something to be enjoyed with others. Eating healthily is something that everyone should be able to enjoy and we hope this book is just another helping hand in making that a reality.

## Mindful Chef customers have reported feeling leaner, being more productive, having more focus and generally feeling healthier.

Foods that are good for you and foods that are good for the environment don't always go hand in hand. Having spent most of our lives growing up in the countryside and next to the coast we have been lucky enough to have access to amazing, fresh, quality food on our doorstep. We believe there is a fundamental connection between how your food is grown and how good it is for you; not to mention its impact on the planet. For this reason it's also been important to us and to Mindful Chef that we use the highest-quality food from ethically-minded suppliers. Suppliers who care not only about the welfare of their animals, but also how their food is grown and what the unintended negative consequences of their farming decisions might be on the world.

In 2015 our main mission was to make healthy eating easy and we really believed in the tangible, positive effects we could have on people's lives through helping them to eat better. Equally important to us was creating a company we could be proud of in years to come. One that we could look back on with our children and say, 'Wow isn't that a great business?'. For that to be true we had to be mindful of our impact on the environment. We knew that recipe boxes could be a brilliant way of helping people be more environmentally conscious by helping them to reduce their own food waste. It's very rare, however, that a company can help an individual and the world around it at the same time. Like many things back then we weren't sure at what level we could achieve this but that was our dream and we set out to accomplish it. As we have grown as a company we have become even more interested in our own impact and the consequences our decisions might have on the world around us. We're now a part of the B Corp collective (see page 28) and on a race to Net Zero by 2030 – 20 years ahead of the Paris Climate Agreement.

Interestingly, our approach to nutrition aligns perfectly with some of those of government bodies, including Public Health England's Eatwell Guide and the World Wide Fund for Nature's (WWF) Livewell principles, which focus on six dietary changes individuals can make for a more positive world – changes such as eating more vegetables, eating a varied diet, wasting less food; and eating less but higher-quality meat and fish.

Both the Planetary Health Diet (see page 22) and the Livewell principles match those of Mindful Chef. We have designed recipe criteria that adhere to the following benchmarks:

- Less meat, better meat.
- No dairy ingredients.
- A variety of natural ingredients and whole foods – nothing processed or refined. No added sugar.
- Only grass-fed beef, free-range chicken and sustainable MSC-certified fish.
- 100% British meat and poultry, and fish only from healthy stocks.
- No food waste.

What we took for granted as being rudimentary recipe guidelines for our chefs to follow are actually fundamentally a better way of eating to reduce one's overall carbon footprint of food. We are the only recipe box company to combine the principles of human health and planetary health when designing our recipes.

# The Planetary Health Diet

The food we eat, and the way it is produced, is damaging both our planet and our health. In 2019, the Eat-Lancet Commission published a report on sustainable food systems. As part of that, they outlined The Planetary Health Diet (PHD), the first study to put forward a way of eating that links human health and environmental sustainability – a diet that is healthy for both people and planet. It explains that we can create a sustainable food system that supplies healthy, nutritious food to a growing population, if we follow certain guidelines. The Planetary Health Diet recommends:

- A predominantly plant-based diet with small amounts. of fish, meat and dairy.
- Eating a variety of fruit and vegetables.
- Focus on unsaturated rather than saturated fats.
- Limited refined grains, highly processed foods, added sugars and starchy vegetables.

# Regenerative Agriculture & Soil Health

We've always liked to think of Mindful Chef as a sustainable business: one that seeks to reduce its impact on the world, give back what it takes and generally do less harm. When we use the terms 'sustainable' or 'sustainability' we're referring to the need to find a balance between existing as a company without depleting natural resources for the future, and promoting social development through a range of different projects.

Every company has an impact on the environment through the ways it operates and the products or services it produces and offers. However, there is a growing understanding among businesses that in order to tackle climate change and other societal issues effectively we cannot focus all of our efforts on sustainability alone. At Mindful Chef we have set ourselves a goal of becoming a regenerative business. This is one that not only serves to benefit its customers but also has a restorative impact on society and the environment. In short, a business that's good for its customers but also truly good for the planet too.

We have been told countless stories by our customers about how eating the Mindful Chef way has helped them achieve specific health goals or helped them feel more energised and healthy. To this end we believe that our products really do have a positive impact on people's day-to-day lives. In 2022 we took this a step further, becoming the first recipe box company in the world to start carbon-labelling our recipes. By giving our customers more insight into the impact of the meals they are eating we believe we can support them in making a conscious effort to reduce their own environmental footprint. To work out the carbon impact of our recipes we did a lifecycle assessment, looking at absolutely everything that goes into growing the ingredients,

to delivering, storing, cooking the recipes and disposing of any waste from the packaging. We then worked with the brilliant brains at Climate Partner to rate the recipes. In order to be classed as low carbon a recipe must generate less than 1.6kg $CO_2e$ per person. This is in line with the WWF's target of reducing diet-related emissions by 20% by 2030, a target set in the aftermath of the Paris Climate Agreement (2015) where countries committed to aim to keep global warming well below 2°C.

# In 2022 we became the first recipe box company in the world to start carbon-labelling our recipes.

Roughly 50% of our weekly recipes are low carbon – and despite what some might think, it isn't just the plant-based recipes that make the selection but often the chicken and fish dishes too. Reducing the amount of carbon we generate is a brilliant way to start thinking not only about how we can fix the environmental problems we have created but also about implementing behavioural changes that will have a net positive impact on the world around us in the future. The carbon-labelling is a great example of an environmental project that can make material positive change for our customers and for Mindful Chef. If everyone were to start eating this way, it could make a huge difference to individual carbon footprints, so when more people select our low-carbon recipes it will reduce our overall carbon impact as a business and help us further on our journey to Net Zero by 2030.

Social projects like our partnership with One Feeds Two (see page 56) show the impact small companies can have on a large scale when placing purpose above profit. But in order to really achieve our goal and be a regenerative business, we have to look at our area of biggest environmental concern – our food and the way it is produced, as well as the impact it has if it is wasted.

## REGENERATIVE AGRICULTURE

Having grown up with many friends involved in farming we know the relentless effort and hard work it takes and how much love and respect goes into the land farmers and growers work. For most farmers their biggest desire is to ensure that this way of life is passed down for generations to come. That said, as populations have grown and the need for convenience and choice has overtaken the sensibilities of seasonality there has inevitably been a change in farming methods in order to cater for that increased demand for food. To survive, many farmers and food suppliers have to play a numbers game: how much yield can they produce in order to satisfy consumer demands and maintain contracts, and how much food can a supplier purchase in order to drive the price lower? Farmers are forced to think about short-term outcomes, rather than the long term health of their land and soil.

Farming across the world has changed substantially since the 1950s. The way we produce food, through intensive agriculture, is not good for us or the planet. Not only is agriculture now responsible for a third of global greenhouse gas emissions, the way we are farming is depleting our soil and the quality of our crops. Poorer soil quality means that the crops are poorer nutritionally as well as leading to other potential problems that directly affect us (see page 35). Climate change and an ever growing global population are placing even more pressure on an already strained system so there needs to be a fundamental change in the way we approach farming and feeding ourselves.

This is where the idea of regenerative agriculture becomes really interesting and will play a huge role not only in reducing the impact of global food production, but in protecting and enhancing the natural assets we depend on.

Reducing the amount of carbon we generate is a brilliant way to start thinking about how we can fix the environmental problems we have created and implement behavioural changes that will have a net positive impact on the world.

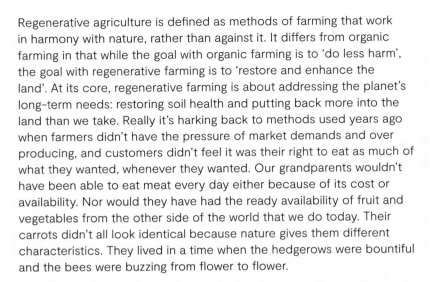

Regenerative agriculture is defined as methods of farming that work in harmony with nature, rather than against it. It differs from organic farming in that while the goal with organic farming is to 'do less harm', the goal with regenerative farming is to 'restore and enhance the land'. At its core, regenerative farming is about addressing the planet's long-term needs: restoring soil health and putting back more into the land than we take. Really it's harking back to methods used years ago when farmers didn't have the pressure of market demands and over producing, and customers didn't feel it was their right to eat as much of what they wanted, whenever they wanted. Our grandparents wouldn't have been able to eat meat every day either because of its cost or availability. Nor would they have had the ready availability of fruit and vegetables from the other side of the world that we do today. Their carrots didn't all look identical because nature gives them different characteristics. They lived in a time when the hedgerows were bountiful and the bees were buzzing from flower to flower.

Many farmers we've spoken to admit that some of their practices over the last 20–30 years have been short-sighted and that in order to continue producing food for years to come they agree there needs to be a change that focuses on reintroducing traditional methods of farming and allowing the land the time and space it needs to recover from the intensive practices of recent years.

It is important to note that many farmers do a brilliant job of producing food under extremely difficult circumstances. In the past few years we seem to have gone from one global crisis to another: a worldwide pandemic, a war in Europe, followed by an energy crisis that has exacerbated the rising cost of living. This is without even mentioning climate change and the increasing stress being placed on farmers due to unusually dry or wet seasons. For our farmers to ensure food has still managed to find its way into shops and on to people's plates has been nothing short of amazing.

While regenerative agriculture can deliver some really wonderful benefits to nature and biodiversity, there are upfront costs and short-term efficiency losses for farmers wanting to implement its practices. We believe in the importance of transitioning to this way of farming, so we're working with our suppliers and supporting them on their regenerative journeys. For example with one of our suppliers we have selected areas of farmland and have started implementing regenerative practices. These include:

- **Minimum tillage:** this a soil conservation system, the main goal of which is to disrupt the soil as minimally as possible with little to no soil turnover. In contrast intensive methods of tillage can change soil structures negatively and degrade soil quality as they dig into the soil as deep as 40cm. Not only is the biological balance of the soil turned upside down but carbon is released from the soil through this process.

- **Cover cropping:** cover crops are grown not to be sold but rather to help support the soil structure in between growing seasons. Their root system and subsequent decomposition of the crop improves water retention, reduces the need for artificial fertilisers and thus boosts the habitat for insects, bees and birds which improves pollination, and increases biodiversity and organic amendment (this is what you add to soil to improve crop yield or quality).

In general businesses need to find more ways of supporting farmers commercially in order to reduce the negative impact of farming and help them integrate practices that can actually give back to the land. Agriculture is often criticised for its negative impact on the environment. However, when we look at it solely as being a negative contributor to the world, we're missing the huge potential that agriculture has as a tool to help us solve the climate crisis, and the answer lies right beneath our feet: in the soil.

## WHY IS SOIL SO IMPORTANT?

Soil is the world's largest terrestrial carbon sink, which means that it takes carbon out of the atmosphere. This is important because an increase in greenhouse gases (like carbon) in the air can have far-ranging environmental effects, such as global warming. In the UK alone our soil stores (sequesters) more than 10 billion tonnes of carbon. Half of this store is found in our peat habitats (some wetlands are made up of a type of waterlogged soil composed of dead and decaying plants called peat) so it is imperative that we keep these important features of our landscape safe. Peatlands are important not only for storing carbon but also as a haven for wildlife, as a water filter and because they act as a form of natural flood prevention. Increased farming is degrading these habitats by converting them to land more suited to agriculture and if we don't start acting soon we could witness disastrous consequences. The good news is that by reducing overuse by humans (for example, the extraction of peat for fuel, gardening and horticulture, such as in compost), preventing the amount of overgrazing by farm animals and supporting farmers to implement regenerative soil management

Regenerative farming is about addressing the planet's long-term needs: restoring soil health and putting back more into the land than we take.

techniques we can protect areas like the UK's peatlands and ensure carbon is kept in the ground.

There is another pressing reason why we need to adopt long-term soil regeneration practices. The earth's soils are being degraded at an alarming rate. According to the WWF half of the world's topsoil has been lost in the last 150 years. This is worrying because not only does it affect crop production – and therefore our ability to produce food, it can also lead to an increase in flooding (eroded soils can't retain water as well as fertile topsoil). We hear first-hand from our suppliers about the problems they are having producing good harvests due to worsening soil quality and irregular weather patterns, which is why many are keen to work with us and introduce more regenerative practices. Without healthy soils we will inevitably find it harder to produce the food necessary for an ever-increasing population.

# Without healthy soils we will inevitably find it harder to produce the food necessary for an ever-increasing population.

Ultimately, healthier soils will result in more nutrient-dense crops, yet the link between soil quality and the health of crops is not spoken about widely enough. In 2021, the *International Journal of Food Sciences* published an article on UK fruit and vegetables highlighting that between 1940 and 2019 there were significant nutritional reductions in iron (50%), copper (49%) and magnesium (10%) in our food. Compounded by busier lifestyles and less time spent outdoors it's no wonder so many of us feel stressed and tired as the nutritional quality of our food also decreases. We think we can all agree that having healthy soil, full of nutrients, will lead to healthier crops which, in turn, are healthier for us as well. We need to stop thinking of soil as something that's out of sight out of mind. Instead we need to think of soil as an opportunity to store carbon, enhance biodiversity and produce healthier crops.

## BIODIVERSITY & WILDLIFE

A large part of regenerative agriculture focuses on increasing biodiversity (having a wide variety of different organisms with an ecosystem) and wildlife across our green spaces. This is important because in order to have an ecosystem that works harmoniously we need all of nature to be working together.

Since the Industrial Revolution, it has been estimated that 50% of the UK's biodiversity has been destroyed. Over the last 20–30 years

farmers have been incentivised to reduce the number of hedgerows on their land which has reduced the amount of space in which animals, insects and bugs can live and therefore flourish. Hedgerows contain wildflowers that attract bees, which in turn pollinate crops; they provide a healthy habitat for animals and other wildlife, which helps to replenish the land and leads to healthier soil. By reintroducing hedgerows and taking care of other wild spaces we can very quickly have a positive impact on these ecosystems.

Soil also holds over a quarter of the planet's biodiversity. A single teaspoon of garden soil may contain thousands of species, millions of organisms and a hundred metres of fungal networks — think worms, ants, slugs and woodlice as well as lots of 'workers' invisible to the naked eye but that we can see under a microscope, such as bacteria or fungal mycelium. The healthier this ecosystem is, the better it can perform its functions. It processes waste organic matter, regulates carbon and water, helps to keep pests at bay and provides raw materials for both plants and humans. To produce healthy crops that provide us with nutritious food, soil biodiversity is essential. The addition and regular use of things like pesticides and herbicides decreases the biodiversity in the soil and reduces the amount of nutrients within it. By using regenerative practices like crop rotation and introducing natural predators to keep pests at bay (rather than using pesticides), we can create a strong ecosystem that ensures healthier biodiversity both above the ground and below it. Nature is so resilient and brilliant at recovering when we give it the opportunity to do so.

By moving towards a more regenerative way of farming and protecting our soils we can effect real positive change. Food and agriculture can play a pivotal role in helping to reduce global greenhouse gas emissions.

We support our suppliers with different projects that can help increase biodiversity, such as adding biodiversity lanes and wildflower strips to farmers' fields. These can also help farmers reduce pest pressure from predatory insects. These types of projects, combined with carefully planned crop and livestock rotations, can help create a complex farm ecosystem that is more resilient to climate change, pests and disease.

By moving towards a more regenerative way of farming and protecting our soils we can effect real positive change. While food production is one of the leading industries driving climate change, food and agriculture can also play a pivotal role in helping to reduce global emissions. If we can support farmers and suppliers to work towards more regenerative agricultural practices and learn to live in better harmony with the planet that is providing so much for us, then we can actually work together to reduce the effects and causes of climate change. To do this we must rethink the way we interact with food at an individual and a corporate level:

- As individuals, we can do this by eating and wasting less and by paying more for quality rather than quantity – for example, by buying less meat but higher quality like free-range or organic where you can be sure of the production methods behind the ingredient. This in turn shifts our reliance on industrial scale food production.
- By supporting our farmers and suppliers which may mean paying more to shop at our local butcher or greengrocer.
- Or as businesses by directly investing in suppliers and regenerative agricultural practices to reduce the impact of their farming.

If we can work collectively on all of these things then we might be able to have a real positive impact on the global crisis we find ourselves in. If we want our children to grow up in a world with abundant sources of healthy food and green landscapes buzzing with life then we need to start looking after our soil better. By focussing more on regeneration and restoring our systems, not just trying to reduce our impact, we can make this a reality.

# Eating Meat & Fish

Healthy food starts with top-quality ingredients and since we founded Mindful Chef we have wanted to provide customers with food from the very best farmers and fishing boats we can find. In the early days this involved us driving around Devon and Cornwall begging farmers to sell us a couple of chicken breasts and take a chance on our idea. We wanted to find people who really cared not only about the land and crops they were farming but the welfare of their animals to produce the highest quality produce.

## WHY QUALITY MATTERS

When we talk about 'quality', we're referring to the way in which the animals have been looked after or the ways in which food has been grown. The meat from animals that have been given time to graze the land and have been properly looked after will be richer not only in flavour, but in nutrients too. Farmers conscious of their impact on the environment will use fewer pesticides and chemicals on their crops, focusing instead on how they can farm in harmony with nature to produce ingredients full of goodness from the ground (for more on this see pages 30–43). Similarly, fishing in a sustainable manner is not only more humane than using large-scale trawlers, for example, because the catch has endured minimal stress; it also produces a better-quality fish to eat.

We think that everyone should be more aware of where the food they're eating comes from and how it arrived on their plates, and that there should be more emphasis on eating less but higher-quality food. If we could make this switch it would pave the way for more sustainable farming and fishing practices, ones that take more time and produce less food but are better for us and the planet.

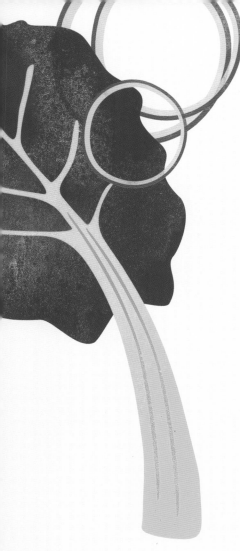

This is most true in the case of meat. Animal welfare varies starkly depending on the conditions in which the animals are reared; the farming methods have different environmental consequences as well. We believe animals should have access to the outdoors and be reared in the most natural way possible. Cattle, for example, have evolved to eat grass; nowadays, however, most farmed cattle are only fed grain and cereals to fatten them up quickly so that they can be sold as soon as possible and be more profitable. Outdoor, grass-fed animals produce meat that is higher in omega-3 fatty acids than meat from grain-fed animals which in turn makes the meat healthier for us. At Mindful Chef we have very strict supplier codes of conduct, predominantly around animal welfare, which we require our suppliers to adhere to. For example, we only use free-range, RSPCA-assured chicken, which ensures that the lives of the chickens are enriched because they're provided with habitats where they are free to roam, which in turn encourages them to exhibit their natural behaviour. All our suppliers are regularly audited to ensure that the highest welfare standards are upheld in order to give the chickens the best quality of life. By having such measures in place we can ensure that our customers are getting food that is not only more nutritious for them, it's better for the animals and for the planet too (to understand more about the different environmental factors resulting from meat farming see pages 51–52). It costs more money to buy better-quality ingredients: free-range chicken breasts aren't cheap but at the same time they shouldn't be. A lot of time, cost and hard work goes into rearing those chickens properly but we have become so accustomed to seeing food at rock bottom prices that there is a disconnect between the animal and the plate of food. This is compounded by the fact that many people feel they need to have meat and fish at every meal, which means that the most cost-effective solutions to source them become very appealing.

We believe meat and fish play an important role in overall health but we do think that everyone could benefit from reducing their reliance on eating them.

What if each of us started to place more emphasis on eating less meat and fish? Could we then direct more of our money towards buying food locally and choosing higher-quality, more sustainable options? That isn't to say we believe everyone should transition to a plant-only diet: we believe meat and fish play an important role in overall health and there are numerous benefits to including them in your diet which we'll delve into further in this chapter. But we do think that everyone could benefit from reducing their reliance on eating them.

# For overall health you don't need to avoid meat completely but it is prudent to be aware of the type of meat you are eating and how much.

You'll remember from the first chapter that our approach to food is based on balance. We prefer to look at overall diet rather than focus on any one food or way of eating. Besides, we believe this approach is more realistic. The environmental argument that everyone should switch to a vegan diet immediately throws all sensibility and human psychology out of the window. Asking individuals to reduce their reliance on meat and fish and eat less of it on a regular basis is not only more realistic but is also more regularly accepted. Human nature suggests that we are extremely resistant to giving up things we deem important to us or are used to. At Mindful Chef, when we introduced our plant-based range of recipes we did not see all of our customers instantly switch to a plant-based box overnight. Nor did we suddenly see the number of plant-based customers overtake our meat and fish box customers. What we did see was a lot of our regular customers increase the amount of plant-based only meals they ordered each week alongside their meat and fish recipe boxes. This is where we believe there is a real, tangible opportunity for society as a whole. If everyone adopted this approach then we could reduce the demand placed on the meat industry and implement better farming practices that negative impact the environment less.

## IS MEAT REALLY BAD FOR US?

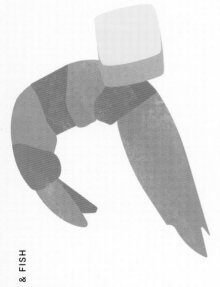

With the rise of veganism globally there has been closer scrutiny over the impact of meat on our health. We've been very clear from the beginning that we believe eating the right types of meat does fit within a healthy diet. Not only do such meats help to build and preserve muscle, which is key to achieving overall health, they're also high in vitamins and minerals. However, eating too much meat, particularly the wrong types of meats, can be problematic. In the western world processed meats, such as sausages, bacon, ham and luncheon meats – those that have been preserved by smoking, curing, salting or adding preservatives – are more readily available and make up a larger part of our diets compared to other populations. Processed meat is classified as Group 1, carcinogenic to humans according to the World Health Organization.

To view this in its full context, we do also need to point out that research has shown that heavy meat eaters who are linked to an

increased risk of various diseases also tend to eat fewer healthy foods. They are likely to eat more processed foods and generally place less emphasis on eating fresh vegetables and fruits (compared to someone who might have transitioned to a vegan diet where their number one priority becomes eating more vegetables and fruits), which means that their overall diet is compromised, regardless of the fact that they meat. For overall health you don't need to avoid meat completely but it is prudent to be aware of the type of meat you are eating, how much, and what else your diet includes.

## IS MEAT BAD FOR THE ENVIRONMENT?

Meat, especially beef, has long been demonised for its impact on climate change. There is no denying that meat (production and consumption) does have an impact on the environment but there is an important difference between the types of meat you can buy and how it has been reared. We've already spoken about types of farming and subsequent environmental impacts and that is of absolute importance when looking at how meat is produced. The clearest distinctions are between intensive farming and smaller independent farms. Intensive farming can involve feedlots, for example, where cows are kept in pens and grown as quickly as possible. In some circumstances the natural landscape may be cleared to create more space for the feedlots, which increases soil degradation and biodiversity loss.

Smaller independent farms that place an emphasis on sustainability and looking after the land, are able to minimise their impact on the environment and can actually benefit it through more natural farming practices.

Smaller independent farms that place a real emphasis on sustainability and looking after the land, are able to minimise their impact on the surrounding environment and can actually benefit it through more natural farming practices. Just allowing cattle to move and graze freely can improve wildlife and soil health. As cattle rotate between fields they move plants and vegetation around, which provides the soil with nutrients. Excrement from the cattle themselves also helps to enrich the soil. Allowing animals and nature to move and live this way helps lead to a thriving habitat.

We discussed earlier the role that soil has to play in carbon sequestration (see page 000); in addition, integrating grazing livestock into a farming system is one of the key principles of regenerative

agriculture, which results in healthier green spaces and more plants. An increase in the number of healthier plants means a higher level of photosynthesis and therefore higher levels of carbon dioxide drawn from the atmosphere. This carbon is then either captured within the plants themselves or in the surrounding soil.

The argument against non-intensive small-scale livestock farms is that the amount of carbon produced per kg of meat is higher than on intensive farms due to the lower quantity of meat produced on the land used. It is true that feedlots fit more animals into a smaller amount of space, however this argument disregards the other environmental benefits of farming in harmony with nature, which improves not only the welfare of the animals themselves but also the soil, the wildlife and biodiversity.

As a society, we have a decision to make. Either we support smaller, less intensive ways of farming that produce – in our opinion – healthier, better-quality meat with other positive effects on the environment, which will mean either paying more for meat and eating less of it; or we continue expecting cheap meat to be on our plate at every mealtime and support the argument that intensive feedlots are necessary to support the population's wants and needs. At Mindful Chef we would prefer our soils to be healthier and for wildlife and biodiversity to be thriving, while eating the very best quality meat available. Which is why we believe the answer lies in eating less but higher-quality meat.

## PLANT-BASED EATING

According to surveys by YouGov and The Vegan Society the number of vegans in the UK quadrupled between 2014 and 2019 to roughly 600,000 people. This is a relatively small amount of the British population. However, another survey carried out in 2021 found that 46% of adults between the ages of 16 and 75 said they were considering reducing their intake of animal products in the future. This is important because it illustrates that there is more awareness and desire to transition to a diet involving less meat and fish, and more people's meals will be predominantly 'plant-based'. Is this healthy though?

The main argument for vegan or plant-based diets is that they reduce the risk of some diseases and are better for the environment. Like many arguments this one is nuanced and has many different layers. It cannot be disputed that including more vegetables or plants in your diet is a good thing. To argue definitively that a vegan diet will reduce your risk of disease is, however, flawed. A key differentiator behind individuals' health is their overall dietary pattern. So a meat eater who has a diet rich in vegetables and fruit and emphasises whole, minimally processed food is more likely to be far healthier than someone eating a highly-processed vegan diet.

A common mistake people make when transitioning to a vegan diet is they only think about the foods they are removing, i.e. meat and fish. They don't spend much time thinking about what they will replace those foods with. Or more importantly, how they will replace the vitamins, minerals and protein found in abundant amounts in meat and fish.

When the transition to a plant-based way of eating is managed correctly, the benefits can be huge and can help individuals lower their saturated fat levels and cholesterol while at the same time increasing daily levels of dietary fibre and other vitamins and minerals important for optimal health. This will only happen as a result of a well-planned plant-based diet that includes a variety of whole, minimally processed foods. Many plant-based meat alternatives, often touted as healthier and better for the environment, aren't always so. A good example is meat-free burgers which often contain more calories and sodium, less protein and the same amount of saturated fat as a normal burger. Producing meat-free burgers and similar products also have their own negative impacts on the environment. Many are made from soy, for example, which is an intensively-grown crop with high demands on resources such as energy, water and chemicals. It is not a clear cut argument between what is right or wrong for the planet.

Ultimately any diet can be healthy or unhealthy and when thinking about what you should be eating there are a lot of things to consider. From both a health and environmental perspective our approach is to ensure you have a balanced approach to nutrition – a diet rich in vegetables, fruits, whole grains, legumes, nuts, good sources of fat and whole, minimally-processed foods (including meat and fish if you wish). We advocate eating high-quality ingredients from suppliers who are farming or fishing in a way that limits their negative impact on the environment, working instead to promote practices that help develop and support soil health, wildlife and biodiversity. If you can balance all of the above you should not only be able to achieve a healthy diet for yourself but one that is also kinder to the planet.

# The Power of a Community

We are big believers in the power of joining forces as a community and that when we all come together we can make real, long-lasting, positive change to the world around us — to people and planet. There are three community initiatives we undertake as a business that we are more proud of than anything else we do.

## One Feeds Two

For every meal we send to our customers we provide a school meal to a child living in poverty through our partner One Feeds Two. The scheme is important because it encourages school attendance and the best way out of poverty for these children is education. At the time of writing Mindful Chef and One Feeds Two have provided over 16 million school meals to children in need. Currently all of our school meals go to children in Malawi and in 2019 we were lucky enough to visit some of the schools and witness first-hand how this project positively impacts these children's lives.

## The Big Mindful Chef Clean-Up

Originally named the Mindful Chef Coast Clean we had to rename this annual event because so many people who weren't based close to the coast wanted to get involved. Nowadays, our little idea to rid some of our coasts of rubbish has grown to be one of the largest single clean-ups in the UK. This year we had almost 4,000 volunteers take part at nearly 400 locations across the UK, collectively picking up more than 160,000 litres of rubbish. This event is a fantastic example of showing the power of a community coming together.

## Reverse Advent Calendar

We also work with food charities closer to home. Every year in the UK we encourage our community to take part in our reverse advent calendar with a twist. Instead of taking food as you would with a traditional advent calendar, customers put food into their box each day of December. We then collect up all of the full boxes of food and deliver them to our food partner. This helps ensure support is given to people in need at this difficult time of year and collectively has a big impact.

## What Can You Do to Help?

You might not be a part of the Mindful Chef community and that's okay, but there are still lots of things you can do on a daily basis which can have a positive impact on the environment and in turn your community. Here are some of our favourite ways to be kind to the planet:

### Buy pre-loved.

From books, to furniture, to clothes, consider buying them second hand.

### Walk more, drive less.

It's also kinder to your mind too (exercise makes your brain release chemicals that make you feel good).

### Don't waste food.

This is probably one of the single best things we can all do (for more on the impact of food waste on the planet see page 35).

### Avoid single-use items.

Use your own shopping bags, coffee cups, cutlery and drinks bottles instead of disposable ones.

### Donate or sell items.

This increases the lifespan of these items and keeps them out of landfill.

### Ditch aluminium foil in cooking.

Foil that has food on it is hard to recycle. If you need to use something, swap it for parchment paper instead.

# Cook's Notes

## COOKING TIMES

At Mindful Chef our ethos is to help you create convenient, simple and healthy meals everyone will enjoy. Because of this, we aim for most of our recipes to be cooked in 30 minutes or less. If a recipe takes longer, this is because the dish might need a little longer to develop flavour or the right texture, so enjoy the process, knowing the result will be totally worth it. To help you create the dish in the quickest time, be sure to prep all your ingredients beforehand, then you'll be ready to go!

## WHICH OIL?

Choosing the right oil is never easy. Deciding what is best for your body, the environment and your recipe can often be a minefield: rapeseed generates the least amount of greenhouse gas emissions, but other oils, such as sunflower, use less water in their production. The key thing to remember is that the impact on the environment depends entirely on the way the oil is produced. To minimise the environmental impact of oil, it is important to buy the best quality you can and try to buy organic. We advocate using rapeseed or olive oil in this book. So long as no pesticides have been used, there is little known significant damage to air, water, land or soil in the production of these oils. They are also lower in trans-fats (bad fats) than most other vegetable-based oils, lowering the risk of heart disease and diabetes. As rapeseed oil has a higher smoking-point than olive, we would also recommend using rapeseed to cook with, and olive oil to dress and finish with, such as in a salad dressing or to drizzle over a risotto.

## WHY ALMOND MILK?

Typically plant-based milks have a lower environmental impact than dairy milk but, like with oil, there are important differences between plant-based milks and their impact on the environment. Throughout the book we suggest using almond milk as this creates the least amount of greenhouse gas emissions during its production and requires less land than other plant-based milks, despite using more water. Unless specified, the choice of plant-based milk or yoghurt won't make a huge difference to the recipe, so go with your preference, just be sure to choose a no-added-sugar option.

## GLUTEN-FREE PASTA?

Every recipe in this book is gluten-free, because we think everyone should be able to enjoy our meals. As a gluten-free company, we strongly believe there is a good alternative for everyone with, making it no reason to miss out on any of your favourite foods or ingredient staples. Throughout this book we recommend alternatives to wheat pasta and noodles. Our favourite is brown rice flour pasta, as it has a mild flavour and chewy texture that is very similar to most traditional pasta types. It is also loaded with fibre, micronutrients and antioxidants, making it a great addition to a balanced diet.

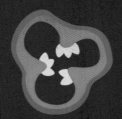

# Recipes

# Spring

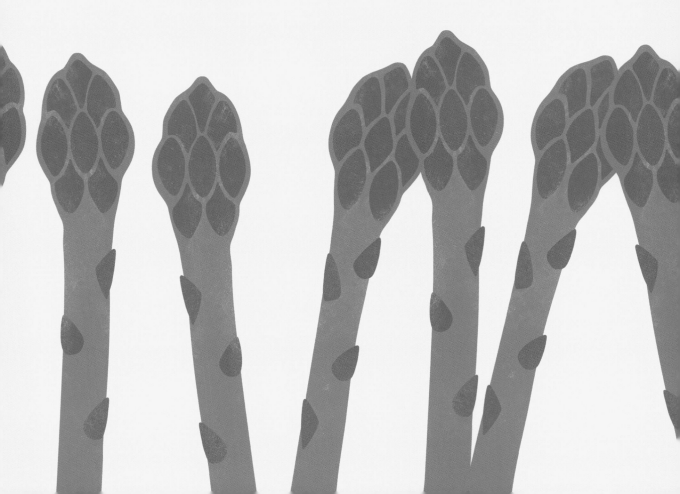

As the days get longer, the natural world begins to buzz into life again following a restful winter. The warmer days allow us to spend more time exploring the beautiful British countryside and it becomes easy to see that it is not just the birds and the bees which have woken up – as the season progresses, hedgerows push beyond their natural boundaries, flowers are in bloom and there is more produce ready to harvest.

The ultimate seasonal treat in spring has to be asparagus – the British season is short so now is the time to make the most of it. Asparagus is as delicious simply pan-fried with a pinch of sea salt as it is in slightly more complex dishes, and you'll find several recipes that celebrate it in this chapter.

Wild garlic is another ingredient we love at Mindful Chef. It can be found in abundance in damp areas of our woodlands and thanks to its distinct smell you'd be hard-pressed to miss it, so head out with your friends, family or on your own for a little foraging expedition. Easier still, wild garlic will be readily available at farmers' markets and independent shops.

Late spring brings the opportunity to harvest the first colourful fruits of the year, like strawberries and rhubarb. Their arrival is a nod to the changing seasons and a first sign that summer is on the horizon. We've championed both of these ingredients in two very different and delicious, healthy desserts (see pages 96 and 98).

# Warm Butter Bean & Chicory Salad

Serves 2

An incredibly versatile and colourful veg salad. Unlike lettuce, chicory has bitter, crisp leaves and is the perfect ingredient to jazz up a midweek salad. Lightly cooking the leaves tames the bitterness and enhances their natural sweetness. Enjoy them at their best from January to March.

1 tbsp olive or rapeseed oil

2 shallots, finely diced

3 garlic cloves, finely chopped or crushed

150g baby plum tomatoes

2 heads of red chicory

1 × 400g tin of butter beans, drained and rinsed

2 tbsp nutritional yeast

80g sugar snap peas

40g rocket

### FOR THE DRESSING

2 tbsp maple syrup

2 tbsp red wine vinegar

2 tbsp Dijon mustard

60g sundried tomatoes in oil, roughly chopped

1   Start by making the dressing. Combine the maple syrup, vinegar and mustard in a large serving bowl, then add the sundried tomatoes.

2   Heat the oil in a medium frying pan over a medium–high heat and add the shallot, garlic and tomatoes. Fry for 3–4 minutes, until the veg begins to soften.

3   Trim the root off the chicory to separate the leaves.

4   Add the butter beans to the pan of tomatoes along with the nutritional yeast and 2–3 tablespoons of water. Cook for another 2–3 minutes then add the sugar snap peas and chicory for a minute to warm them through.

5   Transfer the bean mixture to the bowl of dressing, add the rocket and toss everything to combine. Serve warm.

# Eggs Royale Pancakes with Asparagus & Tartare Sauce

Serves 2

Eggs Royale, a firm British favourite. Here, we have made it perfect for spring, adding asparagus and tartare sauce to turn it from a classic breakfast to an elegant and balanced midweek meal.

75g buckwheat flour

olive or rapeseed oil

150g asparagus, trimmed

160g baby spinach

1 tbsp white wine vinegar

2 large eggs

100g smoked salmon

sea salt and black pepper

½ lemon, cut into wedges, to serve

### FOR THE TARTARE SAUCE

20g pea shoots

20g capers, roughly chopped

20g gherkins, roughly chopped

80g almond yoghurt

½ lemon

2 tsp Dijon mustard

1 Start by making the tartare sauce. Finely chop one third of the pea shoots. Place in a small bowl along with the capers and gherkins, yoghurt, a squeeze of lemon juice and the mustard, to taste.

2 To make the pancakes, place the flour in a bowl and gradually whisk in 150ml water, 1 tablespoon of oil and a pinch of salt. Mix until smooth, adding a little more water if needed until you have a thick pouring consistency.

3 Heat a large non-stick frying pan with 1 teaspoon of oil over a medium heat. Spoon half the batter into the pan and spread it into a thin pancake. Cook for 2 minutes, then flip and cook the other side. Repeat with the remaining batter to make two pancakes. Transfer the pancakes to a plate and cover with foil to keep warm. Boil the kettle and put a medium saucepan of water on to boil.

4 Place the asparagus and spinach in the frying pan and cover with boiling water from the kettle. Bring to the boil and cook for 2–3 minutes, until the asparagus has softened. Drain, then toss with 2 teaspoons of oil and a pinch of salt and pepper.

5 Meanwhile, add the vinegar to the saucepan of boiling water. Bring to a gentle simmer over a medium heat, then create a whirlpool in the pan with a spoon. Break an egg into a mug, lower the mug to the surface of the water, then carefully tip into the middle of the whirlpool. Repeat with the other egg, gently nudging the first one to the side after it starts to solidify. Cook for 4 minutes, until the whites are set, then remove with a slotted spoon.

6 Place the pancakes on plates and top with the spinach, asparagus and smoked salmon. Season the eggs with salt and pepper then place on top of the pancakes.

7 Spoon the tartare sauce over the pancakes and garnish with the remaining pea shoots. Serve the lemon wedges on the side.

## 🍳 Chef's tip

For successful pancakes, make sure:

- you use a non-stick pan
- the pan is hot before you pour in the batter
- the bottom of the pancake is cooked and golden-brown before you flip it

# Jersey Royal & Minted Pea Salad

Serves 2

Peas and mint: the taste of British springtime. Although frozen peas are readily available and just as nutritious, there is nothing quite like enjoying them fresh, when they are still crisp and earthy. Salty ingredients are also a pea's perfect companion. By tossing them with sun-dried tomatoes, we have added a rich, savoury punch to this seasonal salad.

300g Jersey Royal potatoes

300g fresh peas, shelled, or 150g frozen peas

180g Tenderstem broccoli

80g almond yoghurt

2 garlic cloves, finely chopped or crushed

handful of mint, leaves picked and finely chopped

handful of dill, finely chopped

1 tbsp Dijon mustard

1 × 400g tin of butter beans, drained and rinsed

3 radishes, trimmed and thinly sliced

20g sundried tomatoes in oil, roughly chopped

1 tbsp balsamic vinegar

1 tbsp maple syrup

sea salt and black pepper

1   Quarter the potatoes lengthways to create wedges. Place in a medium saucepan of salted boiling water and simmer for 15–16 minutes or until tender, adding the peas and broccoli for the final 3 minutes, then drain.

2   To make the dressing, place the yoghurt, half the garlic, half the mint and dill, and mustard, to taste, in a bowl. Season with salt and pepper and mix well.

3   Mix the butter beans, radishes, sundried tomatoes, potatoes, peas and broccoli together in a large bowl, then add the balsamic vinegar, maple syrup and the remaining garlic, mint and dill. Season well with salt and pepper. Serve drizzled with the yoghurt dressing.

# Asparagus, Lemon & Mint Buckwheat Risotto

Serves 2

Short but sweet, the UK asparagus season usually runs for a mere two months of the year, typically between the end of April and June depending on where you are in the country. Chefs and food lovers describe British asparagus as the best in the world, and we agree it's well worth the wait! Here we pair asparagus with sugar snap peas to add a touch of sweetness to the earthy spears.

½ vegetable stock cube

1 tbsp olive or rapeseed oil

2 brown onions, finely diced

4 garlic cloves, finely chopped or crushed

80g sugar snap peas, halved lengthways

200g asparagus, trimmed and cut into 2–3cm lengths

80g buckwheat

3 tbsp cashew butter

40g almonds, roughly chopped

handful of mint, leaves picked and finely chopped, plus extra leaves to garnish

1 lemon

sea salt and black pepper

1   Heat the oil in a medium frying pan over a medium heat. Add the onions and cook for 6–8 minutes, stirring regularly, until golden brown, then add the garlic for another 2 minutes. Put the stock cube into a jug and cover with 700ml boiling water, stirring to dissolve. Add the buckwheat, stir, and leave for 1 minute, then add the stock and the cashew butter. Allow to simmer for 12–15 minutes, stirring regularly, until the buckwheat is tender with a slight bite. Season with salt and pepper.

2   Add the asparagus and sugar snaps to the buckwheat and cook for a further 4–5 minutes, until softened. Add a little more water if the mixture becomes stiff.

3   Heat a frying pan on a medium heat. Add the almonds and toast for 2–3 minutes, until golden brown. Remove and set aside. Cut the lemon in half. Add the chopped mint and the juice from one of the lemon halves to the buckwheat and stir well. Season with salt and pepper.

4   To serve the risotto, squeeze over the juice from the remaining lemon half, adding it to taste, and garnish with the toasted almonds and mint leaves.

# Roasted Sweetheart Cabbage with Chickpea Madras & Chilli Cashews

Serves 2

Despite being affordable and loaded with nutrients, cabbage gets a bit of a bad rep. Bring out the best in this hardy and versatile brassica, by roasting till crisp and tender. Roasting the cabbage in wedges prevents overcooking and creates a great caramelisation that reveals a little sweetness in this bitter leaf.

1 medium sweetheart cabbage, cut lengthways into 4 wedges

1 tbsp olive or rapeseed oil

1 brown onion, finely chopped

3 garlic cloves

30g creamed coconut

1 × 400g tin of chickpeas, drained and rinsed

2 tsp garam masala

2 tsp ground coriander

2 tsp cumin seeds

1 tsp chilli flakes

1 × 400g tin of chopped tomatoes

200g fresh peas, shelled, or 100g frozen peas

30g cashew nuts, finely chopped

handful of coriander, finely chopped

sea salt and black pepper

1   Preheat the oven to 220°C/200°C fan/gas 7. Line a baking tray with baking paper.

2   Place the cabbage on the lined tray and drizzle with 1 tablespoon of oil. Season with salt and pepper. Roast for 20–25 minutes, until soft and beginning to char.

3   Meanwhile, finely chop or crush 2 of the garlic cloves. Dissolve the creamed coconut in a heatproof jug with 50ml boiling water.

4   Heat a large frying pan with 1 teaspoon of oil on a medium–high heat. Add the onion and cook for 6–8 minutes, until soft and golden. Season with a generous pinch of salt and pepper. Once softened, add the chopped garlic along with the chickpeas, garam masala, ground coriander, cumin seeds and half the chilli flakes. Cook for 2 more minutes.

5   Pour the chopped tomatoes and creamed coconut into the pan and cook for 8–10 minutes, until thickened, then stir in the peas. Cook for 2 more minutes to heat them through. Season to taste.

6   Meanwhile, thinly slice the remaining garlic clove. Heat a small frying pan with 2 tablespoons of oil on a medium–high heat and add the garlic, cashew nuts, remaining chilli flakes and a pinch of salt. Toast for 10 seconds, then remove from the heat.

7   Stir half the coriander into the Madras sauce, then spoon on to the centre of your serving plates. Lay the charred cabbage wedges on top and drizzle over the cashew nuts and their chilli oil. Garnish with the remaining coriander.

# Watercress & Pea Fritters with Lemon Dill Yoghurt

Serves 2

An often-overlooked seasonal leaf, watercress is a fantastic option when trying to shop sustainably. The UK produces some of the best watercress in the world, so reduce your carbon footprint by getting your hands on this nutritious ingredient. High in iron, magnesium and calcium, it's good for you, as well as the planet. Far more interesting than just throwing it in a salad, try it in these crispy pea fritters served with a zesty herb dip.

2 tbsp olive or rapeseed oil

2 brown onions, finely sliced

2 tsp cumin seeds

300g fresh peas, shelled, or 150g frozen peas

100g watercress, roughly chopped, plus extra to garnish

30g mixed soft herbs (we use mint, coriander and flat-leaf parsley), roughly chopped, plus extra to garnish

125g chickpea flour

160g almond yoghurt

2 garlic cloves, finely chopped or crushed

handful of dill, finely chopped

grated zest of 1 lemon

1 preserved lemon

200g baby plum tomatoes, quartered

1 tsp extra virgin olive oil

sea salt and black pepper

1   Heat 1 tablespoon of the oil in a large frying pan over a medium heat and cook the onions for 8–10 minutes, until soft and golden brown. Stir in the cumin seeds, cook for 1 minute more, then add the peas, watercress and herbs. Cook for 1–2 minutes to wilt the watercress, then remove from the heat and set aside to cool.

2   In a mixing bowl, combine the chickpea flour with 125ml water and mix to form a smooth, thick batter. Season with salt and pepper.

3   While the pea and watercress mix is cooling, prepare the lemon yoghurt and a quick tomato salad. Put the almond yoghurt into a small bowl with the garlic and dill. Add the lemon zest, then cut the lemon in half and squeeze in a little juice, to taste. Season with a pinch of salt.

4   To make the tomato salad, halve the preserved lemon and remove most of the pulp using a teaspoon. Finely dice the rind and add. to a bowl with the tomatoes and mix. Add the extra virgin olive oil and a pinch of salt, to taste (careful, preserved lemons can already be quite salty!).

5   Once the pea and watercress mix has cooled slightly, stir it into the chickpea batter.

6   Return the frying pan to a medium–high heat with another tablespoon of oil and spoon in 2 tablespoons of the mixture for each pancake (you'll need to cook them in batches). Cook for 2–3 minutes on each side, until golden brown. Set aside and repeat to get 8–10 fritters in total.

7   To serve, spoon the yoghurt on to each serving plate and place the fritters on top and the tomato salad alongside.

# Chicken Curry
# with Spiced Carrot Salad

Serves 2

We use a lot of carrots here at Mindful Chef. They are colourful, full of nutrients and available all year round. Here, we pair them with a chicken curry, to create texture and use their refreshing sweetness to balance the acidity and richness of the tomato-based sauce.

100g black rice

½ chicken stock cube

2 tsp cumin seeds

2 shallots, thinly sliced

2 tbsp red wine vinegar

300g boneless, skinless chicken thighs, cut in half

1 tbsp curry powder

1 tbsp tomato purée

150g almond yoghurt

handful of coriander, roughly chopped

2 carrots, coarsely grated

1 tsp nigella seeds

1 lime

1 tsp ground coriander

1 tsp olive or rapeseed oil

1   Bring a medium saucepan of salted water to the boil. Add the rice and boil for 30–35 minutes, until cooked, then drain.

2   Dissolve the stock cube in a jug with 200ml boiling water.

3   Heat a medium frying pan on a medium–high heat. Toast the cumin seeds for 1–2 minutes, until fragrant.

4   Make the pickled shallots. Put shallots into a bowl with the vinegar and half the cumin seeds. Set aside.

5   Put the chicken thighs into a bowl with the curry powder, tomato purée and half the yoghurt. Leave to marinate.

6   Meanwhile, in a mixing bowl, combine the coriander, carrot, nigella seeds and ground coriander then grate in the zest of the lime. Cut the lime in half and add the juice from half and the remaining yoghurt and cumin seeds. Mix to combine.

7   Reheat the frying pan with the oil on a medium–high heat. Cook the chicken for 2–3 minutes on each side, until the marinade begins to stick slightly. Add the stock and simmer for 4–5 minutes, until the sauce thickens. Check your chicken is cooked through by cutting a large piece in half; the flesh should be white and the juices running clear. Cook for longer if necessary.

8   Serve the rice with the chicken and carrot salad. Garnish with the pickled shallot and the remaining lime half, cut into wedges.

# Herby Quinoa & Hazelnut Rocket Salad with Grilled Chicken

Serves 2

Rocket is a popular salad leaf, known for its strong peppery flavour — you either love it or hate it. We just can't get enough of it and think it's a match made in heaven paired with pan-fried chicken breast and glazed in sticky sweet honey.

100g quinoa

30g hazelnuts, roughly chopped

2 × 150g skinless, boneless chicken breast

1 tbsp olive or rapeseed oil

2 tbsp clear honey

2 tbsp Dijon mustard

finely grated zest and juice 1 lemon

1 shallot, finely chopped

100g celery, finely chopped

handful of flat-leaf parsley, finely chopped

handful of mint, leaves picked and finely chopped

80g rocket

sea salt and black pepper

1  Bring a large saucepan of salted water to the boil. Add the quinoa and boil for 13–14 minutes, until tender with a slight bite, then drain.

2  Meanwhile, heat a dry frying pan on a medium heat. Toast the hazelnuts for 2–3 minutes, until dark brown. Remove and set aside.

3  Place the chicken breasts between 2 sheets of baking paper and use a rolling pin to bash them into an even, 1cm-thick layer. Rub them with the oil and season with salt and pepper. Heat a medium griddle pan (or frying pan) on a medium–high heat. Add the chicken and cook for 4–5 minutes per side, until golden brown all over.

4  While the chicken is cooking, combine the honey and mustard in a bowl. Add the lemon zest and juice and season with salt. Pour the dressing over the chicken and turn it to coat. Cook for another minute. Check your chicken is cooked through by inserting a skewer into the meat; the juices should run clear. Cook for longer if necessary. Keep the pan on the heat and add 3 tablespoons of water. Bubble for 1 minute, until the liquid thickens slightly, then remove the chicken and transfer it to a board.

5  Put the shallot, celery and herbs into a large mixing bowl. Add the cooked quinoa along with the rocket and the liquid from the chicken pan and stir to combine. Season with salt and pepper and transfer to plates. Slice the chicken and place it on top, then scatter over the hazelnuts and serve.

# Roasted Duck with Rhubarb Compote

Serves 2

A naturally sour vegetable, rhubarb comes into its own when paired with a little sweetness. Here, we cook it in honey to create a sweet but sour compote. The perfect accompaniment to cut through a rich duck breast.

600g large white potatoes, we used Maris Piper, peeled and cut into 3cm chunks

2 carrots, peeled and cut into cm batons

olive or rapeseed oil

2 × 160g duck breasts

100g rhubarb, trimmed and cut into 2cm chunks

25g clear honey

½ tsp ground cinnamon

2 tsp apple cider vinegar

2 tsp cornflour

½ chicken stock cube

150g Savoy cabbage, trimmed and sliced

2 garlic cloves, finely chopped or crushed

sea salt and black pepper

1   Preheat the oven to 240°C/220°C fan/gas 9. Line a large baking tray with baking paper.

2   Place the potato and carrot in the lined tray. Drizzle over ½ tablespoon of oil and season with salt and pepper. Roast for 25–30 minutes until golden, turning halfway through.

3   Heat a large frying pan on a medium–high heat. Add the duck, skin-side down, and cook for 4–5 minutes until crispy. Flip and seal on the other side, then transfer to the tray alongside the vegetables (skin-side up) for the final 8–10 minutes of cooking. When the duck breast is cooked, it should remain quite soft but still spring back when lightly pressed. Check your duck is cooked by slicing the breast in half. It should still be pink in the middle, but if it's too rare for you, return to the oven for a few more minutes. Once done, allow the duck to rest for at least 5 minutes before slicing.

4   Meanwhile, put the rhubarb into a small saucepan on a medium heat with the honey, cinnamon and half the vinegar. Add 75ml of water and simmer for 8–10 minutes, until the rhubarb breaks down and the liquid reduces – you'll have a thick compote.

5   Dissolve the cornflour in a jug with 50ml cold water; crumble in the stock cube and top up with 250ml boiling water. Return the pan used for the duck (with the fat) to a medium–high heat. Fry the cabbage and garlic for 3–4 minutes until beginning to soften. Add the remaining vinegar and the stock mixture. Simmer for 4–5 minutes, until the cabbage is soft and the liquid has thickened slightly.

6   Serve the sliced duck alongside the roasted vegetables and rhubarb compote. Spoon the cabbage on to the plates, leaving the sauce in the pan, then drizzle it over the plate.

# Salmon, Asparagus & New Potato Tray Bake with Sunflower Seed Pesto

Serves 2

Although potatoes are available all year round, it's important to know which varieties are in season if you want to reduce your carbon footprint. Jersey Royals and salad potatoes are at their prime during spring. Sweeter and better at retaining their shape than their larger counterparts, baby potatoes are the obvious choice for roasting in this recipe.

300g baby white potatoes, halved lengthways

½ tbsp olive or rapeseed oil

3 spring onions, trimmed and cut into 2cm pieces

1 Little Gem lettuce, cut lengthways into 6 wedges

130g asparagus, trimmed and cut into 2cm pieces

2 salmon fillets, with skin

sea salt and black pepper

## FOR THE SUNFLOWER SEED PESTO

handful of dill, finely chopped

handful of mint, leaves picked and finely chopped

20g sunflower seeds, finely chopped

2 garlic cloves, finely chopped or crushed

grated zest of 1 lemon, juice of ½, remainder cut into wedges

½ tbsp extra virgin olive oil

1   Preheat the oven to 220°C/200°C fan/gas 7. Line a baking tray with baking paper.

2   Place the potatoes on the lined tray, rub with the oil and season with salt. Roast for 15 minutes.

3   At this point, add the spring onion, lettuce and asparagus to the tray and mix well. Lay the salmon on top, skin-side up, and continue to roast for a further 10–12 minutes, until the salmon is cooked and the potatoes are golden.

4   While the salmon is cooking, make the pesto. Add the chopped dill and mint to a small bowl with the sunflower seeds, garlic, lemon zest and juice and the extra virgin olive oil. Season with salt and pepper then mix well.

5   Remove the salmon from the tray. Toss half the pesto through the roasted vegetables and transfer to serving plates. Top with the salmon and dot the remaining pesto around the plates. Garnish with the lemon wedges.

# Wild Garlic Mussels & Chips

Serves 2

A popular ingredient among foragers, wild garlic is commonly found in the British woodlands between March and June. As well as being delicious, wild garlic has many proven health benefits – it's anti-inflammatory and antibiotic. When not in season, wild garlic can be substituted with chives or spring onion mixed with a little garlic. Serve the mussels with a salad of mixed bitter leaves, for a quick and balanced midweek meal.

300g large white potatoes, we used Maris Piper

1 tbsp olive or rapeseed oil

2 shallots, finely sliced

2 garlic cloves, finely sliced

3 tbsp white wine (optional)

1 lemon, quartered

500g mussels, cleaned (see Chef's tip)

sea salt and black pepper

### FOR THE SALSA VERDE

20g wild garlic, finely chopped

10g mint, leaves picked and finely chopped

10g parsley, finely chopped

2 tsp Dijon mustard

2 tsp capers, roughly chopped

1 tbsp sherry vinegar

2 tbsp extra virgin olive oil

1  Preheat the oven to 220°C/200°C fan/gas 7. Line a baking tray with baking paper

2  Cut the potatoes lengthways into chips. Place in the lined tray, drizzle with ½ tablespoon of oil and season with salt and pepper. Bake for 25–30 minutes, until golden.

3  Meanwhile, put all the ingredients for the salsa verde into a bowl, season with salt and pepper, mix well and set aside.

4  Heat a large heavy-bottomed saucepan with ½ tablespoon of oil over a medium heat. Cook the shallot for 6–8 minutes, stirring occasionally, until softened. Add the garlic and cook for 2 more minutes, then turn up the heat. Add the wine (if using) or 3 tablespoons of water. Bring to the boil, then add the mussels to the pan. Quickly cover with a lid, and cook for 3–4 minutes, shaking the pan occasionally, until all the mussels have opened (discard any unopened shells).

5  Remove the pan from the heat and stir in the salsa verde. Serve the mussels in bowls with the chips and lemon wedges alongside.

## Chef's tip

To clean your mussels, place them in a large bowl filled with cold water and soak them for 15–20 mins. Sort through them, discarding any that are damaged or remain open, even when tapped. Using the back of a knife, pull off the beard and any other fibres on the shell. Once cooked, discard any mussels that have not opened.

# Prawn & Spinach Pesto Potato Salad

Serves 2

Good for more than bulking up a salad or curry, it's time to give this humble leaf a bit of time in the spotlight. You can make pesto from a number of different leaves, but we think spinach is one of the best. Plus, it's a great way to use up any spinach you have in the back of your fridge.

300g baby white potatoes, halved lengthways

100g fresh or frozen peas (200g unshelled pods)

2 large eggs

1 tbsp olive or rapeseed oil

300g raw king prawns

½ lemon, halved

10g dill, roughly chopped

20g capers

20g pea shoots

sea salt and black pepper

**FOR THE PESTO**

30g pine nuts

150g baby leaf spinach

15g basil, leaves picked

1 garlic clove, roughly chopped

20g nutritional yeast

3 tbsp extra virgin olive oil

½ lemon

1  Place the potatoes in a saucepan of salted boiling water. Simmer for 15–18 minutes, until soft, adding the peas for the final 2 minutes. Drain and set aside.

2  Meanwhile, make the pesto. Heat a dry medium frying pan over a medium heat. Toast the pine nuts for 2–3 minutes, tossing regularly, until golden brown. Remove from the heat and set aside.

3  Put the spinach, basil, garlic, nutritional yeast and half the pine nuts into a food processor or blender. Add the extra virgin olive oil and 2–3 tablespoons of water and blend until smooth. Finely chop the remaining pine nuts and stir them through the pesto. Season with a squeeze of lemon juice and some salt and pepper.

4  Bring a small saucepan of water to the boil. Carefully lower the eggs into the pan using a spoon. Boil for 7 minutes, then remove. Run the eggs under cold water, then carefully peel and cut in half.

5  Reheat the frying pan on a high heat with 1 tablespoon of oil. Add the prawns, season with a pinch of salt and fry for 1–2 minutes until pink, then add the juice from one quarter of the lemon and half the chopped dill. Remove from the heat.

6  To assemble, mix the potatoes, peas, pesto, capers and most of the remaining chopped dill together in a mixing bowl and toss.

7  Serve on plates and top with the prawns, soft-boiled eggs, pea shoots and reserved dill. Serve with the remaining lemon quarter, cut into wedges.

 Chef's tip

Use this easy spinach pesto to jazz up any midweek meal. Brighten up your pasta night or stir a few tablespoons through classic mashed potato.

# Hot-Smoked Salmon & Beetroot Pasta Salad

Serves 2

Beetroot is a fantastic ingredient if you're looking to lower your carbon footprint and introduce more veg into your diet. Due to our cool climate, beetroot is grown commercially throughout the UK, so does not have to travel far to get to our shop shelves. Beetroot rarely needs treating with pesticides, making it a very environmentally friendly crop to have on your shopping list. Often considered a winter vegetable, beetroot is actually best in spring, when it is at its sweetest.

300g beetroot, peeled and cut into 2cm cubes

120g gluten-free pasta (we use brown rice penne)

15g walnuts, roughly chopped

80g almond yoghurt

2 tbsp basil pesto (or try our pesto recipe on page 88)

40g rocket

10g dill, three quarters roughly chopped

2 hot smoked salmon fillets, peeled and flaked

sea salt and black pepper

1　Place the beetroot in a large saucepan of salted boiling water. Boil for 20–22 minutes, until soft, then drain and season with salt and pepper.

2　Meanwhile, cook the pasta in a pan of salted boiling water for 7–8 minutes (or according to the instructions on the pack), then drain.

3　Transfer the beetroot to a large mixing bowl and mash to a rough purée. Add the walnuts, yoghurt, pesto, rocket and chopped dill. Season with salt and pepper then mix well.

4　Add the cooked pasta to the bowl and stir to coat it in the sauce. Transfer to serving bowls and serve topped with the salmon and garnished with the remaining dill sprigs.

 Chef's tips

You can either use shop-bought pesto or try our pesto recipe on page 88. If your beetroot still has its leaves attached, keep them – add them to the pasta pan in the final 2 minutes of cooking to pack in even more goodness.

SPRING

# Samphire & Lemon Baked Cod with Pesto Tomatoes

Serves 2

A common sea vegetable, you can forage for samphire yourself. Found near the seashore, samphire grows particularly well in the UK's cooler climate. Best raw or simply cooked, here we roast it with its favourite flavour companion, fish, to make a simple dinner, packed with nutrients.

80g tricolour quinoa (or use plain if that's what you have at home)

1 tbsp olive or rapeseed oil

150g baby plum tomatoes

1 shallot, finely chopped

40g samphire

2 × 150g skinless cod fillets

1 lemon, zest grated

handful of mint, leaves picked and roughly chopped

1 tbsp extra virgin olive oil

80g almond yoghurt

2 tbsp basil pesto (shop-bought or try our pesto recipe on page 88)

15g pea shoots

sea salt and black pepper

1   Preheat the oven to 200°C/180°C fan/gas 6. Bring a medium saucepan filled with salted water to the boil. Add the quinoa and boil for 13–14 minutes, until cooked, then drain.

2   Heat a large ovenproof frying pan with 1 tablespoon of oil on a medium–high heat, then add the tomatoes and half the shallot. Season with salt and pepper. Fry for 2–3 minutes, until beginning to soften.

3   Remove the pan from the heat. Scatter the samphire over the tomatoes, then gently place the cod on top. Add half the lemon zest and season. Bake in the oven for 10–12 minutes, until the fish is cooked through.

4   Return the drained quinoa to the empty saucepan and stir through the mint, remaining shallot and the extra virgin olive oil. Season with salt and pepper.

5   In a small bowl, stir the remaining lemon zest into the yoghurt. Cut the zested lemon in half, add a squeeze of the lemon juice, to taste, then season with salt and pepper. Cut the other lemon half into wedges.

6   Divide the quinoa between two plates and top with the cod. Add the pesto to the pan, stir in the tomatoes, then dot around the cod. Drizzle over the lemon yoghurt; garnish with the pea shoots and lemon wedges.

# Sea Bass with Shallot Purée, Charred Spring Onions & Hasselback Potatoes

Serves 2

A hugely versatile ingredient, humble spring onions can be used for much more than just a garnish. When roasted, they lose their sharp oniony taste and transform into a sweet and succulent side in their own right. Don't bother trimming, you can eat the whole thing except the stringy root, which can easily be bitten off!

300g baby new potatoes

olive or rapeseed oil

4–6 banana shallots (about 250g), roughly chopped

1 bay leaf

½ tbsp maple syrup

100g almond cream

6 spring onions

120g oyster mushrooms, roughly torn into large pieces

2 × 120g sea bass fillets

sea salt and black pepper

1  Preheat the oven to 220°C/200°C fan/gas 7. Line a baking tray with baking paper.

2  Prepare the hasselback potatoes. Cut thin slices into each potato, without going all the way through to the bottom (see Chef's tip below). Place the potatoes in the lined tray, rub with ½ tablespoon of oil and season with salt. Roast for 15 minutes, then remove from the oven.

3  For the shallot purée, heat a medium frying pan on a medium heat and add the shallot and bay leaf. Cook for 15 minutes until completely soft, then add the maple syrup and cook for another 2 minutes. Add half the almond cream and continue to cook for another 4–5 minutes until it coats the shallots. Transfer to a blender and blend, adding the remaining cream a little at a time until the mixture is smooth and silky, then set aside.

4  Peel the outer layer from the spring onions. Add to tray with the potatoes, drizzle with 2 teaspoons of oil and season with salt and pepper. Return the tray to the oven to roast for a further 10–15 minutes, until the potatoes are soft and spring onions are charred and soft through.

5  Meanwhile, heat a large frying pan with 2 teaspoons of oil on a high heat. Add the mushrooms to the pan and cook for 2–3 minutes, until golden brown and softened. Season with salt and pepper.

6  Move the mushrooms to one side of the pan, season the sea bass with salt and pepper. Drizzle another ½ tablespoon of oil into the pan and add the sea bass. Cook for 2–3 minutes on each side, until the skin is golden brown and the flesh is cooked through.

7  To serve, reheat the shallot purée in a small saucepan over a medium heat (if necessary), then spoon on to plates. Place the sea bass on top, and garnish with the charred spring onions and oyster mushrooms. Serve the hasselback potatoes on the side.

 Chef's tip

For an easy way to hasselback your potatoes, sit each spud in the well of a wooden spoon, or in-between two chopsticks, before making your slices. This will prevent you from cutting all the way through to the bottom.

# Rhubarb & Cardamom Crumble

Serves 2

Pretty in pink, this rhubarb and cardamom crumble is a perfect remedy for those spring evenings that still hold a little chill. Coconut sugar gives it a fantastic caramel undertone and really takes the crumble up a level. Plus, with a lower GI than white sugar, it won't give you that post-dessert sugar rush.

### FOR THE FILLING

200g rhubarb, trimmed and cut into 2cm lengths

1 × 200g cooking apple, cored and cut into 2cm cubes

50g coconut sugar

½ tsp vanilla bean paste

½ tsp ground cardamom

### FOR THE CRUMBLE

50g ground almonds

50g coconut sugar

25g gluten-free porridge oats

½ tsp cinnamon

½ tsp ground ginger

50g coconut oil

### TO SERVE

80g coconut yoghurt

1   Preheat the oven to 180°C/160°C fan/gas 4.

2   Put the rhubarb and apple into a small ovenproof dish along with the rest of the filling ingredients. Mix then bake in the oven for 10–12 minutes, until starting to soften.

3   For the crumble, put the ground almonds, coconut sugar, porridge oats and spices into a mixing bowl and stir to combine. Add the coconut oil and rub together to form a breadcrumb texture.

4   Sprinkle the crumble topping over the filling and bake for 25–30 minutes, until the top is dark golden brown and the filling is bubbling. Leave to cool for 5 minutes before serving with a generous dollop of coconut yoghurt.

## Chef's tip

As one of the first fruits we see post-winter, rhubarb is the perfect plant for any novice gardener. You can harvest the stems from early April through to July. Try it out in this crumble, or opt for other seasonal fruits, such as pears or strawberries.

# Elderflower & Lemon Polenta Cake with Instant Strawberry Ice Cream

Serves 8–10

Freezing strawberries is a great way to manage a glut, and we recommend using them to make this super-easy four-ingredient ice cream. The cake is a fancy but fuss-free finale to any meal.

## FOR THE CAKE

150g instant polenta

200g ground almonds

2 tsp baking powder

½ tsp bicarbonate of soda

100ml extra virgin olive oil

200g maple syrup

250ml plant-based natural yoghurt

1 tbsp sugar-free elderflower cordial

grated zest of 2 lemons

## FOR THE DRIZZLE

juice of 2 lemons

100ml sugar-free elderflower cordial

## FOR THE ICE CREAM

125g coconut yoghurt

250g frozen strawberries

1 tbsp maple syrup

1 Preheat the oven to 180°C/160°C fan/gas 4. Line a 23cm springform cake tin with baking paper.

2 To make the cake, mix all the dry ingredients together in a large bowl.

3 In another bowl mix the olive oil, maple syrup, yoghurt and elderflower cordial and beat together until incorporated. Stir in the lemon zest, then add the wet ingredients to the dry. Mix together well.

4 Pour the batter into the lined tin and bake for 45–50 minutes, until coming away from the edges of the tin and golden brown on top.

5 While the cake bakes, make the drizzle. Mix the lemon juice and elderflower cordial together in a small bowl and set aside.

6 Once the cake is out of the oven, prick it all over with a skewer or small knife, then pour all but 2 tablespoons of the elderflower lemon drizzle over the top. Leave to cool before slicing.

7 For the ice cream, add the reserved drizzle to a food processor or blender with the yoghurt, strawberries and maple syrup. Blitz until smooth. Transfer to a serving bowl and serve alongside the cake. Any leftover cake will keep for 4-5 days if stored in an airtight container in a cool place.

# Summer

For us, summer is often spent on the coast with friends and family, enjoying the most of the outdoors and devoting as much time as possible to swimming in our beautiful blue coastal waters. Dipping in and out of the sea and appreciating the balmier evenings inevitably results in less time spent in the kitchen but this doesn't mean dinner cannot be delicious. Now is the time to get creative with lots of ingredients that need minimal cooking to deliver fantastic flavour.

The first courgettes, ripening tomatoes and beans of all sorts arrive thanks to the warmer weather, and fields and allotments are brimming with salad leaves and berries. Cucumbers, fennel, sweetcorn and radishes are at their best in summertime.

There is nothing more reminiscent of childhood and satisfying than going strawberry or raspberry picking in the sunshine then heading home to make the most of this incredible produce. That is of course if the berries have managed to survive the journey home and not been gobbled up by the pickers en route. We have two simple recipes that showcase these summer ingredients. Our Italian Tomato & Strawberry Salad on page 104 is a healthy, easy option for those nights when you want a lighter dinner to enjoy outside. Or our Raspberry Frangipane with Chocolate Avocado Mousse (see page 134) is absolutely delicious and perfect for a summer evening.

# Kohlrabi Chickpea Cherry Salad with Pistachios

Serves 2

A great dish for a hot summer evening, this low-effort salad delivers impressive results without tieing you to the kitchen. We use a zingy lemon dressing to soften this crunchy vegetable, which has a similar flavour to a turnip, and use a little natural sugar to balance out its underlying earthiness.

2 kohlrabi bulbs, peeled and coarsely grated

1 tbsp olive or rapeseed oil

2 garlic cloves, finely chopped or crushed

1 × 400g tin of chickpeas, drained and rinsed

handful of dill, finely chopped

100g cherries, pitted and halved

2 tbsp tahini

3 tbsp maple syrup

grated zest and juice of 1 lemon

handful of pea shoots

20g pistachio nuts, roughly chopped

sea salt and black pepper

1   Place the kohlrabi in a sieve and mix it with a good pinch of salt. Set aside for 5–10 minutes, then squeeze out the liquid.

2   Heat a medium frying pan with 1 tablespoon of oil on a medium–high heat. Add the garlic and fry for 2 minutes, then add the chickpeas. Warm through for 2–3 minutes, then stir in the dill.

3   Put the kohlrabi and cherries into a large mixing bowl along with the tahini, maple syrup, lemon zest and juice. Season with salt and pepper.

4   Stir the warm chickpeas into the kohlrabi and serve garnished with the pistachios and pea shoots.

 Chef's tip

Don't waste the kohlrabi leaves; they are edible and delicious. Cook them as you would kale. Fry, boil or steam them, then serve as a super-healthy side.

# Italian Tomato & Strawberry Salad

Serves 2

When in season, British strawberries are abundant – but they're not just for desserts! This salad balances the sweetness of strawberries with salty olives and tangy vinegar, to create a satisfying, savoury dish. Perfect for supper and a healthy choice for those with a sweet tooth.

1 × 400g tin of chickpeas, drained and rinsed

1 tbsp olive or rapeseed oil

1 yellow pepper, deseeded and thinly sliced

3 beef tomatoes, roughly chopped

100g strawberries, hulled and quartered

1 shallot, finely chopped

30g pitted black olives, halved

handful of basil, roughly chopped

2 tbsp basil pesto (shop-bought or try our pesto recipe on page 88)

1 tbsp nutritional yeast

1 tbsp red wine vinegar

1 tbsp extra virgin olive oil

15g pine nuts

sea salt and black pepper

1   Preheat the oven to 240°C/220°C fan/gas 9. Line a baking tray with baking paper.

2   Add the chickpeas and peppers to the lined tray, drizzle with 1 tablespoon of oil and season with salt and pepper. Bake for 20–25 minutes until the pepper is soft and the chickpeas are slightly crispy.

3   Meanwhile, place the tomatoes, strawberries, shallot, olives, basil, pesto, nutritional yeast and vinegar in a mixing bowl. Drizzle over the extra virgin olive oil and season with salt and pepper. Mix well and leave to marinate until the chickpeas are ready.

4   Heat a small frying pan on a medium heat. Toast the pine nuts for 2–3 minutes, tossing regularly, until golden brown. Remove from the pan and set aside.

5   Stir the roasted pepper and chickpeas into the salad, top with the toasted pine nuts and serve.

# Roasted Tomato & Tofu Pasta with Pesto Dressing

Serves 2

Nothing quite compares to juicy red tomatoes picked at their prime during the peak of the British summer. In this spread, we've stuck to a classic pairing: sweet baby plum tomatoes with basil and balsamic vinegar, jazzing the dish up a little with protein to create a truly satiating and balanced meal.

280g firm tofu

1 red onion, cut into 1cm wedges

2 tsp olive or rapeseed oil

handful of basil, roughly chopped

handful of flat-leaf parsley, roughly chopped

2 tbsp basil pesto (shop-bought or try our pesto recipe on page 88)

1 tbsp balsamic vinegar

2 tbsp maple syrup

juice of 1 lemon

100g Tenderstem broccoli, trimmed, each stem cut into three horizontally

250g baby plum tomatoes, cut in half

120g gluten-free pasta (we use black bean spaghetti)

20g walnuts, roughly chopped

sea salt and black pepper

1   Preheat the oven to 240°C/220°C fan/gas 9.

2   Drain the tofu, pat it dry with paper towel and cut it into 1cm cubes. Place in a roasting tin with the onion wedges and toss with 1 teaspoon of oil. Season with salt and pepper and roast for 20 minutes.

3   Meanwhile, make the pesto dressing. In a small bowl stir together the chopped herbs, pesto, vinegar, maple syrup and lemon juice, then season to taste with salt and pepper.

4   After 20 minutes, add the broccoli and tomatoes to the roasting tin. Drizzle with 1 teaspoon of oil and season with salt and pepper. Roast for a further 10 minutes.

5   Cook the pasta in a large saucepan of salted boiling water over a high heat according to the instructions on the pack, then drain.

6   Add the pasta to the roasting tin along with the dressing and toss well to coat. Serve in bowls and top with the chopped walnuts.

# Aubergine with Muhammara-Style Dip & Butter Bean Hummus

Serves 2

Here, we make aubergine pop by coating it in maple syrup and pomegranate molasses. It's served with muhammara, a traditional Syrian dip of red pepper, walnuts, lemon, pomegranate molasses and chilli, for a Middle Eastern-inspired feast that really puts plants centre stage.

1 aubergine, halved lengthways

2 red peppers, halved, deseeded and cut into 3cm sqaures

3 tsp olive or rapeseed oil

½ tbsp smoked paprika

100g quinoa

1 × 400g tin of butter beans, drained and rinsed

1 tbsp tahini

2 tbsp pomegranate molasses

2 tbsp maple syrup

200g baby plum tomatoes, cut in half lengthways

40g sundried tomatoes in oil, finely chopped

20g walnuts, finely chopped

1 tbsp extra virgin olive oil

handful of flat-leaf parsley, roughly chopped

handful of dill, roughly chopped

sea salt and black pepper

1   Preheat the oven to 240°C/220°C fan/gas 9. Line a baking tray with baking paper.

2   Cut a criss-cross pattern into the exposed aubergine flesh (being careful not to cut the skin). Place on the lined tray, skin-side down, along with the peppers. Drizzle with 2 teaspoons of oil and season with three-quarters of the smoked paprika and a pinch of salt and pepper. Roast for 20 minutes.

3   Place the quinoa in a saucepan of salted boiling water over a high heat and boil for 13–14 minutes, until cooked, then drain.

4   To make the hummus, place the butter beans and 200ml of water in a medium saucepan set over a medium–high heat. Bring to the boil, then reduce the heat to medium and simmer for 6–8 minutes, until the beans are completely soft and the liquid has reduced by two thirds. Remove from the heat, add the tahini and season with salt and pepper. Using a potato masher, mash to a smooth hummus, adding a splash of water if it's a little dry.

5   Mix half of the pomegranate molasses and half of the maple syrup in a small bowl, then spread the mixture over the flesh of the aubergine. Add the baby plum tomatoes to the tray, drizzle with 1 teaspoon of oil and season with salt and pepper. Return the tray to the oven to cook for another 10–12 minutes, until the veg is soft.

6   Remove the peppers from the tray, chop finely and transfer to a bowl. Mix with the sundried tomatoes and half of the walnuts. Stir in the remaining pomegranate molasses, maple syrup, smoked paprika and the extra virgin olive oil. Season to taste.

7   Stir the parsley, dill and roasted tomatoes through the drained quinoa and season with salt and pepper.

8   Serve the butter bean hummus on plates with the muhammara-style dip spooned on top. Add the aubergine half and the herby quinoa. Garnish with the remaining walnuts.

# Cauliflower & Cashew Nut Mole with Refried Black Beans

Serves 2

Cauliflower is a hearty, earthy veg that is a great blank canvas when cooking. By charring the cauliflower and pairing it with chilli and lots of herbs, we have packed this dish full of flavour and made the impressive brassica the star of these delicious tacos.

1 cauliflower, cut into florets, leaves removed

1 × 200g tin of sweetcorn, drained and rinsed

1½ tbsp olive or rapeseed oil

1 brown onion, finely chopped

3 garlic cloves, finely chopped or crushed

1 × 400g tin of black beans, drained and rinsed

handful of coriander, finely chopped

handful of flat-leaf parsley, finely chopped

handful of tarragon, leaves stripped and finely chopped

2 tbsp nut butter (we like cashew)

1 lime, cut in half

½ tbsp extra virgin olive oil

1 red chilli, finely chopped (remove the seeds for less heat)

2 spring onions, thinly sliced

6 soft corn tortillas

sea salt and black pepper

1   Preheat the oven to 240°C/220°C fan/gas 9. Line a baking tray with baking paper.

2   Place the cauliflower florets and sweetcorn on the lined tray and drizzle with ½ tablespoon of oil; season with salt and pepper. Roast for 15–20 minutes, until the cauliflower is soft and beginning to char.

3   Heat a medium saucepan with 1 tablespoon of oil on a medium heat and cook the onion for 5–7 minutes, stirring occasionally, until softened. Add the garlic and cook for another 2 minutes. Transfer half of the onion and garlic to a mixing bowl. Add the beans to the remaining onion and garlic in the pan. Add 150ml water and simmer on a medium heat for 10 minutes, until most of the liquid has evaporated. Roughly mash and set aside.

4   Add the herbs to the mixing bowl with the cooked onion and garlic, keeping back a little of the coriander for garnishing, then stir in the nut butter, the juice from half of the lime, the extra virgin olive oil and 1–2 tablespoons of water. Season with salt and stir well.

5   Heat a large frying pan on a high heat, then toast three tacos for 30 seconds on each side, then remove and keep warm in a clean tea towel. Repeat with the remaining tacos.

6   Reheat the beans on a low heat if necessary, transfer to a serving dish, then garnish with the chilli, remaining coriander and the spring onion. Serve the beans with the cauliflower, tacos and the remaining lime half cut into wedges.

# Smoky Prawn & Black Rice Salad

Serves 2

Courgettes are a fantastic example of a low-waste veg. You can eat the flesh, the skin, the seeds, and even the beautiful flower on top. Keeping the courgettes raw gives this salad a lovely crunch and freshness, showcasing them at their best.

100g black rice

2 courgettes, shaved into ribbons with a peeler

2 spring onions, thinly sliced (keep the whites and greens separate)

handful of flat-leaf parsley, finely chopped

40g rocket

200g cooked cold-water prawns

6 black garlic cloves

2 tbsp clear honey

¼ tsp chilli flakes, or to taste

1 tbsp red wine vinegar

80g almond yoghurt

1 tbsp extra virgin olive oil

1 tsp smoked paprika

2 red peppers, deseeded and thinly sliced

sea salt

1   Place a large saucepan of salted boiling water over a high heat, add the rice and boil for 30–35 minutes, until cooked, then drain.

2   Meanwhile, add the courgette ribbons, spring onion greens and parsley to a large mixing bowl along with the rocket and prawns. Set aside.

3   To make the dressing, use the flat of a knife to mash the garlic into a paste and add it to a small bowl. Add the honey and chilli flakes, to taste, and stir well to make a smooth paste, then add the vinegar, yoghurt, extra virgin olive oil and a pinch of the paprika. Set aside.

4   Heat a medium frying pan with 2 tablespoons of oil over a medium–high heat. Fry the peppers and the spring onion whites for 8–10 minutes, stirring regularly, until very soft. Season with salt, add half the remaining paprika and continue to fry for 2 minutes.

5   Add the cooked peppers and spring onions to the salad along with half of the dressing and toss to coat.

6   Spread the rice over serving plates and top with the salad. Drizzle the remaining dressing over the salad, garnish with the remaining paprika and serve.

 Chef's tip

When buying courgettes, look for firm, shiny and unblemished fruit. If they feel spongy, this means they're past their prime and should be avoided. Dark green courgettes are the most familiar variety, but look out for white or yellow courgettes to liven up your cooking.

# Sea Bass, Fennel Slaw & Za'atar Potatoes

Serves 2

Raw fennel makes a refreshing addition to any summer dish, bringing a bright anise crunch. In this recipe, we harmonise its subtle liquorice flavour with mint and grape to create a balanced and cooling salad. It's the perfect accompaniment to delicate sea bass.

400g baby white potatoes, cut in half

2 tbsp olive or rapeseed oil

1 fennel bulb, trimmed and finely sliced

1 cucumber, shaved into ribbons

50g seedless red grapes, cut in half

handful of mint, leaves picked and roughly chopped, plus a few extra leaves to garnish

1 lemon

10g pistachio nuts, roughly chopped

2 tsp za'atar

2 × 120g sea bass fillets, with skin

sea salt and black pepper

1   Preheat the oven to 240°C/220°C fan/gas 9. Line a baking tray with baking paper.

2   Place the potatoes in the lined tray. Drizzle with ½ tablespoon of oil, season with salt and pepper, then roast for 20 minutes.

3   Put the fennel, cucumber and grapes into a mixing bowl then squeeze in most of the juice from half the lemon and season with salt. Add the mint and half the pistachios. Squeeze in the juice from the other half of the lemon, mix well and set aside.

4   After 20 minutes, remove the potatoes from the oven and lightly crush with the back of a fork, drizzle with another ½ tablespoon of oil and sprinkle over the za'atar. Roast for a final 5–8 minutes, until soft and golden.

5   Season the sea bass with salt. Heat a medium non-stick frying pan with 1 tablespoon of oil on a high heat, then cook the fillets, skin-side down, for 3–4 minutes until the skin is golden brown. Flip and fry for another 2–3 minutes, until cooked (see Chef's tip). Squeeze in a little more lemon juice and remove from the heat.

6   Place the potatoes and fennel salad on serving plates with the sea bass on top. Sprinkle over the remaining pistachios and the mint leaves.

 Chef's tip

For best results when frying sea bass, make sure to get your oil nice and hot before laying your fish in the pan skin-side down. Make sure the skin is golden before flipping, and to prevent over-cooking watch the flesh turn gradually white. As soon as it is all the same colour, remove from the heat.

# Cajun Chilli Con Carne Loaded Fries with Zingy Chilli Salsa

Serves 2

A blast of spice, we have combined the flavours of the deep American South with British summer produce in this knock-out chilli dish. Unknown to many, chillies grow well in the UK from mid-summer to autumn, and just as easily on your kitchen windowsill. The more you pick, the more they'll grow. So pick'em and freeze'em to enjoy British chillies all year round.

300g sweet potato

2 tsp olive or rapeseed oil

1 chicken stock cube

1 red onion, finely chopped

1 red pepper, deseeded and cut into 2cm squares

300g minced turkey

30g tomato purée

2 tsp Cajun spice

2 garlic cloves, finely chopped or crushed

200g passata

1 × 400g tin of kidney beans, drained and rinsed

80g almond yoghurt

sea salt and black pepper

**FOR THE CHILLI SALSA**

240g mixed cherry tomatoes, cut into quarters

1 lime

1 red chilli, finely diced (remove the seeds for less heat)

1   Preheat the oven to 240°C/220°C fan/gas 9. Line a baking tray with baking paper.

2   Leaving the skins on, cut the potatoes into fries. Place on the lined tray and drizzle with 1 teaspoon of oil. Season with salt and pepper. Bake for 20–25 minutes, until soft in the middle and golden all over.

3   Meanwhile, make the chilli. Dissolve the stock cube in a jug with 100ml boiling water.

4   Heat a medium frying pan with 1 teaspoon of oil on a medium–high heat. Add the onion and peppers and season with salt and pepper. Cook for 10–12 minutes, stirring occasionally, until soft and golden, then add the turkey and cook for another 4–5 minutes. Add the tomato purée, Cajun spice and garlic. Cook for 2 minutes more, then add the passata, beans and stock. Cook for 8–10 minutes, until the liquid has thickened slightly.

5   To make the salsa, put the tomatoes into a bowl with the juice from half the lime and the chilli. Add a pinch of salt and mix well.

6   Serve the fries topped with the turkey. Spoon the tomato salsa on top and drizzle over the yoghurt. Cut the leftover lime into wedges and serve on the side.

# Pork Loin, Egg & Chips
# with Homemade Tomato Ketchup

Serves 2

Putting a mindful spin on 'ham, eggs and chips', this is a comforting classic with a seasonal twist. By swapping the ham for pork loin, we turn this high-salt, highly-processed pub classic into a protein- and vitamin-rich meal. It's made even better by using summer tomatoes in delicious homemade ketchup which is as easy as throwing the ingredients into a pan and letting them simmer away while you prepare the rest of the dish.

400g baby white potatoes, quartered lengthways

2 tbsp olive or rapeseed oil

2 shallots, finely chopped

300g baby plum tomatoes

1 tbsp tomato purée

1 tbsp red wine vinegar

2 tbsp clear honey

1 tbsp tamari

¼ tsp ground cinnamon

2 pork loin steaks

2 large eggs

200g peas (fresh or frozen)

1 tarragon sprig, leaves stripped and finely chopped

sea salt and black pepper

1   Preheat the oven to 200°C/180°C fan/gas 6. Line a baking tray with baking paper.

2   Place the potatoes on the lined tray, drizzle with ½ tablespoon of oil then season with salt and pepper. Bake for 20–25 minutes.

3   Place the shallot in a medium saucepan over a medium heat along with the tomatoes, tomato purée, vinegar, honey, tamari and cinnamon. Season with salt and pepper, add 75ml water then bring to a simmer and cook for 15–18 minutes until the tomatoes have broken down and reduced to a thick sauce.

4   Meanwhile, heat a medium frying pan with 1 tbsp oil over a medium–high heat. Add the pork steaks and season with salt and pepper. Fry for 3–4 minutes on each side until golden brown. Check the pork is cooked through by inserting a skewer into the thickest part of the meat; the juices should run clear. Cook for longer if necessary. Remove from the pan and leave to rest for a few minutes.

5   Wipe the frying pan clean and return to a medium–high heat, add another ½ tablespoon of oil, then crack in the eggs and fry them for 2–4 minutes until the white has set and the yolk is cooked to your liking. Season with salt and pepper.

6   Place the peas in a small saucepan of salted boiling water over a high heat. Boil for 2–3 minutes then drain. Stir the tarragon through the peas with a pinch of salt and pepper. Serve the peas alongside the pork steaks and potato wedges. Add an egg to each plate and a generous serving of tomato ketchup.

 Chef's tip

Use this ketchup as a base recipe and adjust it to your taste by adding:

- chilli flakes
- garlic powder
- smoked paprika
- curry powder
- dried seaweed flakes

# Broad Bean Smash with Spiced Lamb & Lemon Yoghurt

Serves 2

1 lemon

100g almond yoghurt

2 garlic cloves, peeled

40g rocket

150g peas, fresh or frozen

1.5kg broad beans, in their pods, podded, or 300–400g podded and skinned (see Chef's tip)

20g flaked almonds

1 tbsp rapeseed or vegetable oil

2 × 150g lamb leg steaks

2 tsp ground coriander

2 tsp cumin seeds

pinch of chilli flakes, plus extra to garnish

handful of dill, roughly chopped

sea salt and black pepper

 Chef's tip

Need some help podding then skinning your beans? Follow these simple steps:

- To remove the beans from their velvety pods run your finger along the furry inside to push the beans out.
- Bring a small saucepan of water to the boil. Cook the beans for 2 minutes, then drain and place in a bowl of ice-cold water to cool.
- Pop the bright green beans out of their leathery grey skins.

The British broad bean season runs from April to September, but they are at their finest during the height of summer. Freshly picked broad beans have a velvety flesh and are a creamy protein-packed addition to any dish. A fantastic way to practise mindfulness, ensure to leave enough time to pod your beans. If you use small beans you don't necessarily need to skin them as well, as they're soft enough; larger beans' skins can be tougher and may need to be skinned (see Chef's tip). This dish is perfect for lunch or a light supper; just add a handful of boiled potatoes for a more substantial meal.

1   Grate the zest of the lemon and add to a small bowl with the yoghurt. Mix, then set aside.

2   Put the garlic cloves into a small food processor with the rocket, peas and two thirds of the broad beans. Cut the zested lemon in half and add the juice from one half to the processor, season with salt and pepper and blitz to a chunky purée.

3   Heat a frying pan over a medium heat. Add the almonds and toast for 2–3 minutes, until golden, then remove from the pan.

4   Return the frying pan to a medium–high heat with ½ tablespoon of oil. Season the lamb steaks with the ground coriander and a little salt and cook for 3–4 minutes on each side for medium, or 5–6 minutes for well done. The meat should be blushing pink when medium and have no pink when well done. Leave to rest while you cook the remaining beans.

5   Return the now-empty frying pan with ½ tablespoon of oil on a medium–high heat. Add the cumin seeds and a pinch of chilli flakes, to taste, and toast for 1 minute, then add the remaining broad beans with a splash of water and warm through for 1 minute before removing from the heat. Season with half the dill, salt and a squeeze of lemon juice.

6   Slice the lamb against the grain (see the Chef's tip on page 127). Scoop the broad bean smash on to serving plates and scatter over the whole spiced beans. Top with the sliced lamb, lemon yoghurt, remaining dill and a few chilli flakes, if wished.

# Roasted Radishes with Lamb, Ranch Dressing & Pea Shoots

Serves 2

While crunchy and delicious when raw, here we switch things up by roasting the radishes in a little oil and serving them hot. You can use any mixture of soft herbs to make the ranch dressing. We have suggested a few but this is a great recipe to use up what you may already have in your fridge or garden.

60g radishes, trimmed and cut in half lengthways

300g baby white potatoes, cut in half lengthways

2 garlic cloves, skin on

3 tsp olive or rapeseed oil

15g pine nuts

2 × 150g lamb leg steaks

1 lemon

sea salt and black pepper

40g pea shoots, to garnish

### FOR THE RANCH DRESSING

juice of ½ lemon

handful of mint, leaves finely chopped

handful of dill, finely chopped

handful of chives, finely chopped

1 tsp Dijon mustard

80g almond yoghurt

 Chef's tip

The 'grain' refers to the muscle fibres, or the lines you see running in one direction across the meat. Muscle fibres cause meat to be tough. By cutting across the grain, you shorten the fibres, making the steak easier to chew and therefore more tender and juicy.

1   Preheat the oven to 220°C/200°C fan/gas 7. Line a baking tray with baking paper.

2   Place the radishes and potatoes in the tray. Add the unpeeled garlic cloves, toss with 2 teaspoons of oil and season with salt and pepper. Roast for 25–30 minutes until the potatoes are golden brown and tender, removing the garlic cloves after 15 minutes.

3   Meanwhile, make the ranch dressing. Grate the zest of the lemon, set it aside for later, then cut the lemon in half. Peel the roasted garlic, then use the flat of a knife to mash it to a paste. Put half of the chopped herbs into a small bowl and add the mashed garlic, mustard, yoghurt and the juice from half the lemon. Mix well and season with salt and pepper.

4   Heat a frying pan over a medium heat and toast the pine nuts for 2–3 minutes, tossing regularly, until golden brown. Remove from the pan and set aside.

5   Reheat the frying pan with 1 teaspoon of oil over a medium–high heat. Season the lamb steaks with salt, then place in the pan. Cook the steaks to your liking: 3–4 minutes on each side for medium or 5–6 minutes on each side for well done. The meat should be blushing pink when medium and have no pink when well done. Remove the meat from the pan and leave to rest for 2 minutes, then slice against the grain (see Chef's tip).

6   Remove the tray of potatoes and radishes from the oven and toss through the lemon zest and remaining herbs. Serve the vegetables with the lamb, drizzle over the ranch dressing and garnish with the pine nuts and pea shoots.

# Sticky Green Beans
# with Flat-Iron Steak & Rice

Serves 2

With roots packed with soil-fertilising bacteria, green beans are a particularly earth-friendly crop that we think deserves some limelight. We've put a Chinese twist on this traditional legume, glazing it in tamari, honey and sesame oil, to really make the flavours sing.

100g brown rice

300g green beans, trimmed

1 tbsp olive or rapeseed oil

2 flat-iron steaks

2 garlic cloves, finely sliced

pinch of chilli flakes

1 tsp rice wine vinegar

2 tbsp tamari

1 tbsp clear honey

2 tsp sesame oil

2 radishes, thinly sliced then sliced again into thin strips

handful of coriander, roughly chopped

10g white sesame seeds

sea salt and black pepper

1   Bring a large saucepan of salted water to the boil on a high heat. Add the rice and boil for 25–30 minutes, until cooked, then drain.

2   Heat a dry frying pan on a medium–high heat. Add the green beans and turn the heat down to low. Cook for 10–15 minutes, stirring occasionally, until blackened and slightly softened.

3   Meanwhile, heat a frying pan with 1 tablespoon of oil on a medium–high heat. Season the steaks with salt and pepper and cook for 2–3 minutes on each side for medium–rare, or 3–4 minutes for medium–well done. The meat should be blushing pink when medium and have no pink when well done. Add the garlic and chilli flakes, to taste, for the final minute of cooking, then remove from the pan and leave to rest while you make the dressing.

4   In a small bowl combine the vinegar, tamari, honey and sesame oil.

5   Slice the steak against the grain (see Chef's tip on page 127). Add the dressing to the pan of beans, then add the sliced steak and garlic, along with any resting juices. Stir well to coat the steak and beans with the juices.

6   Stir the coriander and sesame seeds through the rice. Serve the rice alongside the cooked beef and beans, garnished with the radish.

# Beef Larb & Black Rice Salad

Serves 2

Our take on a classic Thai dish, beat the summer heat with this finger-licking recipe. Sweet lettuce leaves serve as wraps here, the perfect vehicle to cool this spicy, aromatic stir-fried beef salad.

100g black rice

3 radishes, trimmed

1 cucumber, halved lengthways and thinly sliced into half moons

60g cashew nuts, roughly chopped

1 tbsp olive or rapeseed oil

300g minced beef

4 garlic cloves, finely chopped or crushed

2cm chunk of ginger, finely grated or chopped

1 red chilli, finely chopped (remove the seeds for less heat)

1 tbsp clear honey

3 tbsp tamari

handful of coriander, finely chopped

2 limes, grated zest and juice of 1, the other cut into wedges to serve

handful of mint, leaves picked and roughly chopped, plus a few whole for garnishing

1 Little Gem lettuce, leaves separated

sea salt and black pepper

1   Bring a large saucepan of salted water to the boil. Add the rice and boil for 30–35 minutes, until cooked, then drain and rinse under cold water to cool.

2   Put the radishes, cucumber and cashew nuts into a mixing bowl and mix well.

3   Heat a large frying pan with 1 tablespoon oil on a high heat. Add the minced beef and season with salt and pepper. Cook for 8–10 minutes until browned, using a spoon to break it up.

4   Once the meat is browned all over, add the garlic, ginger and half the chilli. Cook for 1 minute on a medium heat, then add the honey and tamari. Cook for 1 more minute, until the liquid coats the meat, then stir in half the coriander and add the lime juice to taste (you're aiming for a balance of sweet and sour). Transfer to a serving bowl, and garnish with the remaining coriander.

5   Finally, add the lime zest, chopped mint and remaining red chilli to the rice and stir through. Lightly season with salt and transfer to a serving bowl.

6   Fill the lettuce leaves with the beef mince, crunchy cucumber, radish and cashew nuts. Serve with the black rice and lime wedges.

# No-Bake Vegan Cherry Cheesecake

Serves 4

Blink and you'll miss it. Cherry season in the UK is a very short one, but with a booming cherry industry that is known for producing first-class fruit, we always try to make the most of it. Vanilla goes particularly well with ripe cherries. Use them here to make the perfect topping to this moreish cheesecake.

**FOR THE FILLING**

200g cashew nuts

300g vegan cream cheese

75ml plant-based yoghurt (we use coconut)

50ml maple syrup

1 tbsp vanilla extract

juice of 1 lemon

**FOR THE BASE**

150g pecan nuts

150g pitted dates

sea salt

**FOR THE TOPPING**

1 tbsp cornflour

500g cherries, pitted

50ml maple syrup

½ tsp ground cinnamon

1   Put the cashews into a large bowl, cover with boiling water and leave to soak for 1 hour. Line a 15 × 20cm baking dish with baking paper.

2   Meanwhile, make the base. Place the pecan nuts and dates in a food processor with a pinch of salt and blitz to a coarse crumb. Pack the crumb into the lined baking dish to form an even layer on the bottom. Chill in the fridge while the cashews soak.

3   For the filling, drain the cashews and add them to a blender with the cream cheese, yoghurt, maple syrup and vanilla extract. Add all but 1 tablespoon of the lemon juice and blend until smooth. Spoon the mix over the base and freeze for 2 hours, until stiffened but still soft.

4   For the topping, in a small saucepan dissolve the cornflour with 100ml water. Add the cherries and maple syrup, the remaining tablespoon of lemon juice and the cinnamon. Put the pan over a medium–low heat and simmer for 8–10 minutes, until thick and bubbling. Leave to cool to room temperature, then spread it over the top of the cooled cheesecake. Chill for another 1 hour, then serve.

# Raspberry Frangipane with Chocolate Avocado Mousse

**Serves 2, with leftovers**

In desserts, raspberry really benefits from being paired with nutty flavours to soften the tart fruit. Here the sweet almond sponge does just that. Topped with the creamy and rich chocolate mousse, there is nothing not to love.

## FOR THE MOUSSE

1 ripe avocado, halved and stoned

1 ripe banana

2 tbsp cacao powder

50ml maple syrup

½ tbsp vanilla extract

## FOR THE FRANGIPANE

50g vegan butter

50g coconut sugar

1 large egg

grated zest of 1 lemon

50g ground almonds

25g vegan dark chocolate, roughly chopped

½ tbsp vanilla extract

10 raspberries

## TO SERVE

handful of berries (we like a mixture, but you can use any you have)

10g toasted coconut chips

1   Scoop out the avocado flesh and add to a blender, along with the banana, cacao powder, maple syrup and vanilla extract. Blend until smooth. Transfer to a freezerproof bowl and place in the freezer for 2–3 hours to set.

2   When the chocolate mix is almost frozen, preheat the oven to 200°C/180°C fan/gas 6.

3   To make the frangipane, in a bowl beat the butter and sugar together using a wooden spoon until pale and smooth, then beat in the egg. Add the lemon zest, then add the ground almonds, chocolate and the vanilla extract and mix well. Place the raspberries in the bottom of 2 ovenproof ramekins, then spoon the almond mixture over the top.

4   Place the ramekins on a baking tray and bake for 25–30 minutes, until the top is golden brown and slightly hardened. Remove from the oven, leave to cool for a few minutes, then top with a scoop of the mousse, the berries and coconut chips and serve.

 Chef's tip

We recommend making the most of summer fruits and serving any leftover chocolate mousse with a handful of mixed berries piled on top. It will keep well in the fridge for up to 3 days.

# Autumn

If you're anything like us, you begin this season by keeping your fingers crossed for an Indian summer when, if you throw on a sweater, you can still enjoy dining al fresco. But there can be no doubt about the many joys of autumn, and those cooler evenings spent in the kitchen bring much happiness as we make the most of the fruit and vegetables on offer.

The colder weather means that we start gravitating towards heartier dishes like soups, stews and bakes and there is a plethora of produce to choose from which lends itself well to these. Crops such as pears, plums, apples, squash and leeks are all ready for harvesting. Not just for dessert, plums can be a brilliant addition to main courses as you'll see from our Pork Loin with Roasted Plums & Ginger Noodles recipe on page 165.

Fresh horseradish is also readily available in the UK in autumn and provides a much needed hot, peppery flavour during these colder months. It pairs extremely well with beetroot as you can experience for yourself in our Beet & Quinoa Salad with Horseradish Crusted Hake recipe on page 154.

# Pickled Celery & Celeriac Salad with Wholegrain Mustard Dressing

Serves 2

Available year-round, celery is often hidden, used in the base of soups or stocks. We think this recipe provides a unique alternative, making it the star of the show. By lightly pickling it, we use celery's savoury, citrusy properties to accentuate the sweetness of the rest of the dish.

1 celeriac, peeled and cut into 2cm cubes

olive or rapeseed oil

20g walnuts

120g celery, thinly sliced

3 tbsp maple syrup

3 tbsp apple cider vinegar

2 tsp wholegrain mustard

2 tbsp extra virgin olive oil

handful of flat-leaf parsley, roughly chopped

1 eating apple, cored and cut into matchsticks

1 × 400g tin of cannellini beans, drained and rinsed

sea salt and black pepper

1   Preheat the oven to 230°C/210°C fan/gas 8. Line a baking tray with baking paper.

2   Place the celeriac on the lined tray, drizzle with 1 tablespoon of oil and season with salt and pepper. Roast for 20–25 minutes, until soft and golden.

3   Meanwhile, add the walnuts to another baking tray and toast in the oven for 4–5 minutes, until browned and fragrant, then set aside.

4   Place the celery in a small saucepan over a medium–high heat with 2 tablespoons of the maple syrup, 2 tablespoons of the cider vinegar, 1 teaspoon of oil and a pinch of salt. Bring to the boil, then remove from the heat and set aside to pickle.

5   To make the dressing, whisk the mustard, extra virgin olive oil and the remaining tablespoon of maple syrup and of vinegar in a small bowl. Season with a pinch of salt.

6   Add a pinch of parsley to the pickled celery. Add the apple, beans, cooked celeriac, walnuts and remaining parsley to a large mixing bowl and toss with the dressing.

7   Arrange the salad on plates and top with the pickled celery.

## Chef's tip

We love a quick pickle and recommend using this pickling recipe again with:

- thinly sliced onions, cucumbers or chilli peppers
- carrot ribbons
- whole cherry tomatoes

# Blackberry & Banana Pancakes

Serves 2

High in fibre and rich in vitamins C and K, blackberries are an easy and delicious way to support the immune system and bone growth. The perfect fruit to add to your breakfast in the autumn, they are also a healthy way to satisfy your sweet tooth.

150g vegan cream cheese

2 lemon thyme sprigs, leaves stripped and finely chopped, plus a few extra leaves to decorate

3 tbsp maple syrup

2 medium-sized ripe bananas

2 eggs, beaten

2 tbsp porridge oats

2 tbsp ground flaxseed

2 tbsp ground almonds

150g blackberries

2 tbsp coconut oil

1   In a bowl stir together the cream cheese, chopped thyme and 2 tablespoons of the maple syrup.

2   Mash the bananas in a medium bowl. Add the eggs and mix using a fork.

3   Add the oats, flaxseed and almonds. Add half the blackberries and mash them a little. Stir well until you have a semi-smooth mix.

4   Heat a frying pan on a medium heat with ½ tablespoon of the coconut oil and spoon in 2 tablespoons of the mixture for each pancake (you'll need to cook them in batches, adding more oil to the pan for each batch). Cook for 2–3 minutes on each side, until golden brown. You should get 6–8 pancakes in total.

5   Serve the pancakes with a generous scoop of the thyme cream cheese, a handful of the remaining berries, a scattering of thyme leaves and a drizzle of the remaining maple syrup.

# Warm Butternut Hummus & Pear Salad

Serves 2

A dip usually associated with the warmer months, we have created a hummus using an autumnal gourd to make it seasonal and even more vibrant. Full of fibre and rich in vitamin C, butternut squash elevates this dish from 'just a salad' to a filling and satisfying midweek meal.

1 small butternut squash, peeled, seeds removed, flesh cut into 2cm cubes

1 × 400g tin of chickpeas, drained and rinsed

2 carrots, peeled and cut lengthways into 3–4 long wedges

2 pears, cored and cut lengthways into 6 wedges

200g Tenderstem broccoli

2 tsp olive or rapeseed oil

handful of coriander, finely chopped, plus a few extra leaves to garnish

3 garlic cloves, finely chopped or crushed

2 tbsp tahini

1 tbsp dukkah

1 tbsp pumpkin seeds

sea salt and black pepper

1  Preheat the oven to 240°C/220°C fan/gas 9. Line a baking tray with baking paper.

2  Place the squash in a large saucepan of salted boiling water. Simmer for 20–25 minutes, until very soft, then drain.

3  Meanwhile, put half the chickpeas into a lined baking tray. Put the remaining chickpeas into a mixing bowl.

4  Add the carrot and pear to the tray with the chickpeas. Drizzle over the oil and season with salt and pepper. Roast for 10 minutes, then add the broccoli. Continue roasting for another 10–15 minutes, until the veg are golden brown and soft.

5  Add the cooked squash to the bowl with the chickpeas, then add the coriander, garlic and tahini. Season with salt, then use a potato masher to mash the mixture into a coarse hummus.

6  Serve the squash hummus topped with the warm chickpeas and vegetables. Garnish with the dukkah, pumpkin seeds and coriander leaves.

 Chef's tip

You can jazz up your hummus all year round by experimenting with other vegetable flavour combinations. We recommend giving beetroot and roasted peppers a go.

# Creamy Garlic Mushrooms with Brazil Nut Crumb & Rosemary Fries

Serves 2

A great source of nutrients for those on a plant-based diet, mushrooms are one of the few non-animal sources of B and D vitamins, as well as being high in fibre to keep you feeling fuller for longer. Here we marry them with a garlicky cream sauce, making this a hearty but healthy midweek meal, perfect for those chilly autumn nights.

400g white potatoes (we like Maris Piper, King Edward or early autumn)

2 tbsp olive or rapeseed oil

½ vegetable stock cube

400g mixed wild mushrooms, cleaned and trimmed

2 shallots, finely chopped

4 garlic cloves, finely chopped or crushed

200ml plant-based cream (we use cashew cream)

80g spinach

40g Brazil nuts

4 tbsp ground almonds

2 rosemary sprigs, leaves stripped and finely chopped

sea salt and black pepper

1   Preheat the oven to 220°C/200°C fan/gas 7. Line a baking tray with baking paper.

2   Cut the potato into thin fries. Place them on the lined tray, drizzle with 1 tablespoon of the oil then season with salt and pepper. Bake in the oven for 25–30 minutes, until golden brown. Once the fries are out of the oven turn the grill to high.

3   Meanwhile, dissolve the stock cube in a jug with 150ml boiling water. Heat a medium saucepan with 1 tablespoon of oil on a high heat. Add the mushrooms and fry for 2–3 minutes until golden. Add the shallot and garlic with a pinch of salt and cook for 2 minutes. Add the cream and stock then simmer for 4–6 minutes until the sauce has thickened, then stir in the spinach and allow to wilt down. Season with salt to taste.

4   Roughly chop the Brazil nuts to form a chunky crumb then mix with the ground almonds and a pinch of salt in a small bowl. Transfer the mushroom mixture to a baking dish and top with the nut crumb. Grill for 2–3 minutes, until the nuts are golden brown (keep an eye on them to make sure they don't burn).

5   Toss the rosemary with the cooked fries and serve with the creamy mushrooms.

# Black Garlic Tempeh & Sweetheart Cabbage Bake

**Serves 2**

For such a simple ingredient, black garlic is a culinary superhero as well as being good for brain function, immunity and heart health. Made by ageing an ordinary garlic clove, it is a gamechanger when cooking, adding a uniquely complex savoury but sweet flavour to any dish. Although available in most supermarkets, black garlic can be easily substituted with a normal garlic clove, garlic powder or paste.

200g tempeh, cut into 1cm cubes

½ tbsp smoked paprika

2 tbsp maple syrup

1 tbsp tamari

1 tbsp olive or rapeseed oil

1 shallot, finely chopped

120g celery, finely sliced

150g sweetheart cabbage, trimmed and finely sliced

½ vegetable stock cube

6 black garlic cloves (or see Chef's tip), peeled

40g sundried tomatoes in oil, cut into quarters

20g raisins

1 × 400g tin of butter beans, drained and rinsed

handful of flat-leaf parsley, finely chopped

100g almond yoghurt

30g flaked almonds

sea salt and black pepper

1   Preheat the grill to high.

2   Put the tempeh into a bowl with the paprika, maple syrup and tamari. Season with salt and pepper and toss to coat.

3   Heat a medium ovenproof frying pan with ½ tablespoon of oil on a medium–high heat. Add the tempeh and fry for 3–4 minutes, tossing regularly, until golden brown. Remove from the pan and set aside.

4   Return the pan to a medium–high heat with ½ tablespoon of oil. Add the shallot and celery, fry for 2 minutes, then add the cabbage and fry for another 3–4 minutes, until golden brown in places.

5   Dissolve the stock cube in a jug with 250ml boiling water. Use the flat of a knife to mash the garlic into a paste, then stir it into the stock along with the sundried tomatoes and raisins.

6   Add the beans to the pan, then pour in the stock, add the tempeh and boil for 2–3 minutes, until the stock has reduced to a thick gravy, then stir the parsley and yoghurt into the sauce and simmer for a further 1 minute.

7   Remove the pan from the heat, scatter the almonds over the top and place under the grill for 2–3 minutes, until they turn golden brown (keep an eye on them – they toast quickly). Divide between plates and serve.

## Chef's tip

You may have some black garlic cloves left over from this recipe but you can use them in the Duck with Blackberry Balsamic Sauce recipe on page 162.

# Beet & Quinoa Salad
# with Horseradish Crusted Hake

Serves 2

Part of the brassica family, fresh horseradish is a far more versatile ingredient than the jarred, store-cupboard staple might suggest. A fiery root, horseradish is best paired with fish that needs a little zing and in this recipe, it adds just that, cutting through the buttery-fleshed hake and making it the perfect accompaniment to the earthy beetroot salad.

200g beetroot, peeled, each beet cut into 8 wedges

4 tsp olive or rapeseed oil

1 red onion, cut into 8 wedges

80g quinoa

3 garlic cloves, finely chopped or crushed

2cm chunk of horseradish, peeled and finely grated

3 tbsp ground almonds

handful of thyme sprigs, leaves stripped and finely chopped

2 × 150g skinless hake fillets

20g capers, roughly chopped

grated zest of 1 lemon

40g mixed salad leaves

sea salt and black pepper

1   Preheat the oven to 240°C/220°C fan/gas 9. Line two baking trays with baking paper.

2   Put the beetroot and onion into a lined tray with 2 teaspoons of oil. Season with salt and pepper, toss to coat and roast for 30 minutes, until the beetroot is soft.

3   Meanwhile, bring a large saucepan of salted water to the boil. Add the quinoa and boil for 13–14 minutes, until cooked, then drain. Leave to cool.

4   Mix the garlic, horseradish, ground almonds and 2 teaspoons of oil in a bowl with half the thyme and a pinch of salt and pepper. Put the fish into the other lined tray and spread the horseradish mix all over the top of the fillets. Roast for the final 10–12 minutes of the beetroot's cooking time until cooked through and golden brown on top.

5   Once the beetroot and onion are ready, remove the tray from the oven, add the capers, lemon zest and the remaining thyme and toss everything together. Just before serving mix the salad leaves into the quinoa and transfer to serving plates. Top with the roasted veg, followed by the fish. Cut the lemon into quarters and serve alongside the fish.

# Cod with Cheesy Creamed Leeks & Crispy Capers

Serves 2

Part of the allium family, leeks have a mild sweetness and are incredibly versatile. Although available year-round, they are at their best between September and March. Serve the leeks alongside flaky tender cod and some crispy salty capers for texture and you've got a delicious, dairy-free feast.

300g large white potatoes (we like Maris Piper or King Edward), peeled and cut into 2cm cubes

½ tbsp extra virgin olive oil

5 tarragon sprigs, leaves stripped and roughly chopped

½ vegetable stock cube

2 tbsp olive or rapeseed oil

2 leeks, thinly sliced

2 garlic cloves, finely chopped or crushed

5 thyme sprigs, leaves stripped and roughly chopped

1 tbsp nutritional yeast

150g vegan cream cheese

2 × 150g cod fillets, skin on

20g capers

80g kale, leaves stripped from their stalks and roughly chopped

sea salt and black pepper

1   Place the potatoes in a saucepan of salted boiling water. Simmer for 15–17 minutes until cooked through then drain. Return to the pan, mash with the extra virgin olive oil and season with salt and pepper, then stir in the chopped tarragon.

2   While the potatoes are cooking, dissolve the stock cube in a jug with 200ml boiling water. Heat 1 tablespoon of oil in a medium saucepan on a medium–high heat. Add the leeks and garlic and cook for 5 minutes, until softened, then add the stock, thyme and yeast. Boil for 5 minutes, until reduced slightly, then add the cream cheese and season to taste with salt and pepper.

3   Season the cod with salt and pepper. Heat a large non-stick frying pan with 1 tablespoon of oil on a medium heat. Add the cod skin-side down and fry for 4–5 minutes. Carefully flip the fish and add the capers, then cook for another 4–5 minutes, until the cod is cooked through and the capers are crispy.

4   Set the cod aside and add the kale to the same frying pan. Cook for 2–3 minutes, until wilted, then season with salt.

5   Place the leeks and mashed potato on plates and top with the kale, cod and crispy capers.

# Iranian Chicken & Herb Noodle Soup

Serves 2

Celebrate the last of summer's ripe green beans with this Iranian-inspired soup. Simmered with handfuls of fresh herbs, spinach and golden turmeric, this vitamin K-rich meal is good for the blood and the bones – a delicious dish, perfect for those early September days.

2 tsp olive or rapeseed oil

1 brown onion, finely sliced

1 chicken stock cube

300g skinless, boneless chicken breast, diced in 3cm pieces

3 garlic cloves, finely chopped or crushed

1 tsp ground turmeric

handful of flat-leaf parsley, finely chopped

handful of fresh dill, half finely chopped

100g green beans, trimmed

40g baby spinach

100g brown rice noodles

20g walnuts, roughly chopped

1 lemon, halved

150g almond yoghurt

sea salt and black pepper

1   Heat the oil in a large frying pan over a medium heat and cook the onion for 7–10 minutes, stirring occasionally, until golden brown and soft.

2   Dissolve the stock cube in a jug with 350ml boiling water.

3   Add the chicken, garlic and turmeric to the pan and continue to cook for 3 minutes, turning occasionally. Add the stock to the pan, along with the parsley, chopped dill and green beans. Simmer for 3–5 minutes, until the beans are cooked, then stir in the spinach.

4   Meanwhile, bring a pan of salted water to the boil. Add the noodles and gently separate them with a fork. Boil for 3–4 minutes, then drain, rinse well, then add them to the chicken broth.

5   Stir in half the walnuts and season with salt and pepper, then add the juice from half the lemon, to taste. Divide the noodle broth between two bowls and serve garnished with the yoghurt, remaining walnuts, dill sprigs and the remaining lemon, cut into wedges.

# Glazed Pigeon, Cumin-Roasted Carrots & Lentils

Serves 2

A high-protein, low-fat meat option, pigeon is also one of the most common wild birds in Britain, making it a very sustainable dietary choice. This tender bird is best cooked quickly over a high heat and in this dish, its natural rich, earthy flavour is combined with the sweetness of a pomegranate molasses glaze.

4 tsp olive or rapeseed oil

2 shallots, finely chopped

4 garlic cloves, finely chopped or crushed

100g green lentils

300g sweetheart cabbage, trimmed and finely sliced

1 tbsp cumin seeds

2 tbsp dukkah

4 carrots, peeled and cut lengthways into quarters

1 chicken stock cube

4 × 40g pigeon breasts

2 tbsp pomegranate molasses

handful of flat-leaf parsley, roughly chopped plus a few extra sprigs to garnish

sea salt and black pepper

1   Preheat the oven to 240°C/220°C fan/gas 9. Line a baking tray with baking paper.

2   Heat a medium frying pan with 2 teaspoons of oil on a medium heat and cook the shallot for 3–4 minutes, until softened, then add the garlic along with the lentils and cook for 1 minute, then add the cabbage, half the cumin seeds and half the dukkah and cook for another 2 minutes.

3   Dissolve the stock cube in a jug with 900ml boiling water. Pour the stock into the pan and boil for 18–20 minutes, until the lentils are soft and only a little liquid remains.

4   Meanwhile, put the carrots into the lined tray. Toss with the remaining cumin seeds, 1 teaspoon of oil and some salt and pepper, then roast for 20–25 minutes, until soft and golden brown.

5   Heat a medium frying pan with 1 teaspoon of oil on a medium–high heat. Season the pigeon breasts with salt and pepper then place in the pan. Cook until golden brown – as a guide cook 2–3 minutes on each side for pink or 4–5 minutes on each side for well done. Add the pomegranate molasses for the final 1–2 minutes, turning the pigeon to coat. Remove fromthe pan and leave to rest for a few minutes before slicing each breast in half lengthways.

6   Scrape any remaining liquid from the pigeon pan into the lentils, then stir in the parsley. Season the lentils with salt and pepper, to taste, then transfer to bowls. Arrange the carrots and pigeon on top of the lentils, then scatter over the remaining dukkah and garnish with parsley sprigs.

# Duck with Blackberry Balsamic Sauce & Boulangère Potatoes

Serves 2

A ubiquitous autumnal ingredient, available in hedgerows between the months of August and October, blackberries are the perfect way to add natural sweetness to dishes. We've paired the berries with the umami flavour of black garlic to create a delicious drizzle for duck breasts.

1 chicken stock cube

2 tbsp olive or rapeseed oil

1 brown onion, finely sliced

2 garlic cloves, finely sliced

400g white potatoes (we like King Edward or Maris Piper), sliced as thinly as possible

2 tbsp olive or rapeseed oil

2 × 160g duck breast fillets, with skin

90g blackberries

2 tbsp clear honey

1 tbsp balsamic vinegar

6 black garlic cloves, mashed to a paste using the back of a knife

160g baby spinach

pinch of ground nutmeg

sea salt and black pepper

## Chef's tip

Just like steak, it is very important to let your duck rest after cooking. The meat continues to cook once removed from the pan and, as the term might suggest, leaving it allows the protein time to relax and reabsorb all of its delicious juices. Allowing enough time for resting will give you a succulent, moist duck breast every time.

1  Preheat the oven to 220°C/200°C fan/gas 7. Line a baking tray with baking paper.

2  Dissolve the stock cube in a jug with 200ml boiling water. Heat the oil in a large frying pan over a medium heat and fry the onion for 4–5 minutes, until softened, then add the fresh garlic and cook for 2 minutes. Add the potato slices and fry for another 5 minutes, until warmed through, then pour in the stock and bring to a boil.

3  Transfer the potato mixture to a 15 × 20cm baking dish, arranging the potato slices on top of one another. Season with salt and pepper and bake for 30–35 minutes, until the potatoes form a crisp golden layer on top, are soft in the middle and the stock has almost evaporated.

4  Meanwhile, season the duck breasts with salt. When the potatoes have about 25 minutes left of cooking, heat a medium frying pan on a medium–high heat. Add the duck, skin-side down, and cook for 4–5 minutes, until the skin is crisp. Flip and cook for 1–2 minutes, until the meat is browned on the outside. Transfer the duck to the lined tray, skin-side up, and bake for 8–10 minutes (set the pan with the duck fat aside). Remove the tray and leave to rest for 5 minutes before slicing (see Chef's tip).

5  Put the blackberries, honey, vinegar, black garlic and 2 tablespoons of water into a small saucepan. Place on a medium heat and simmer for 8–10 minutes, until the blackberries have softened and the sauce has thickened.

6  Reheat the frying pan with the duck fat on a medium heat. Add the spinach, nutmeg and a pinch of salt. Cook for 2–3 minutes until wilted.

7  To serve, scoop the boulangère potatoes on to plates, add the duck and spinach and spoon over the blackberry sauce.

# Pork Loin with Roasted Plums & Ginger Noodles

Serves 2

Despite their short season, in the UK plums grow in abundance. Fibre-dense and one of the juiciest stone fruits around, they belong in much more than just your fruit bowl. Here, we use the tang from plums to cut through a sweet and salty Asian-inspired noodle sauce.

1 small butternut squash
(about 400−600g)

2 tbsp olive or rapeseed oil

2 × 150g pork loins

80g brown rice noodles

2 plums, halved, stoned, each cut into 6 wedges

2cm chunk of ginger, grated or finely chopped

2 tbsp clear honey

grated zest and juice of 1 orange

1 tbsp red wine vinegar

20g watercress

1 tbsp sesame oil

sea salt

1   Preheat the oven to 180°C/160°C fan/gas 4. Line a baking tray with baking paper.

2   Peel the butternut squash and reserve the long strips of skin. Halve and cut the squash into 1cm-thick slices, discarding the seeds. Place the butternut skin and slices on the lined tray and toss with 1 tablespoon of oil and a good pinch of salt. Cook for 10−12 minutes until the skins are golden and crisp, then remove them from the tray.

3   Turn the oven up to 240°C/220°C fan/gas 9. Roast the squash for a further 15−20 minutes, until soft and golden.

4   Meanwhile, season the pork with salt. Heat a large frying pan with 1 tablespoon of oil on a medium−high heat. Add the pork and cook for 4−5 minutes on each side. When the pork is cooked through (check by piercing the meat with a skewer; the juices should run clear), remove from the pan and leave to rest for 5 minutes.

5   Bring a medium saucepan of salted water to the boil. Add the noodles, gently separate with a fork and boil for 3−4 minutes, until cooked, then drain and rinse well.

6   Return the pork pan to a medium heat and add the plums, cut-side down, and the ginger. Cook for 2−3 minutes, until the plums are golden, then add the honey, the orange juice and zest to taste, and 3 tablespoons of water. Cook for 1−3 minutes until the plums have softened slightly and the sauce has thickened. Remove from the heat and add the vinegar.

7   In a large bowl, toss the cooked slices of squash with the noodles, plums and their sauce. Transfer to plates and top with the pork, watercress and squash skin crisps. Drizzle over the sesame oil.

# Za'atar Lamb, Quinoa & Rainbow Carrots

Serves 2

Rubbed in Middle-Eastern spice and served with quinoa, this recipe shows that lamb can be used for more than just a Sunday roast. Perfect for a simple yet nutritious midweek meal, we've used lamb leg, packed with high-quality protein and rich in many other essential vitamins.

1 tbsp za'atar

olive or rapeseed oil

2 × 150g lamb leg steaks

200g rainbow carrots, peeled and halved widthways then cut into batons

1 red onion, cut into 2cm cubes

2 tsp ground coriander

½ chicken stock cube

80g quinoa

15g flaked almonds

100g rainbow chard, cut into 3cm pieces

handful of flat-leaf parsley, finely chopped

½ lemon

sea salt

1   Preheat the oven to 220°C/200°C fan/gas 7.

2   Mix the za'atar in a bowl with 2 teaspoons of oil and a pinch of salt. Coat the lamb steaks with the za'atar and leave to marinate.

3   Meanwhile, place the carrots and onion on a baking tray, with 2 teaspoons of oil and the ground coriander. Season with salt and toss to coat. Roast for 25–30 minutes, until the carrots are soft.

4   Bring a large saucepan of salted water to the boil. Add the stock cube and quinoa and boil for 13–14 minutes, until cooked, then drain.

5   Heat a medium frying pan on a medium heat. Toast the almonds for 2–3 minutes, until golden brown. Remove from the pan and set aside.

6   Put the frying pan back on a medium–high heat with 1 tablespoon of oil. Season the lamb steaks with salt. Add to the pan. As a guide cook for 3–4 minutes on each side for medium; 5–6 minutes for well done. Remove from the pan and leave to rest while you finish the rest of the dish.

7   Put the pan on a medium heat and add the chard stems and leaves. Fry for 1 minute, then add 3 tablespoons of water and steam for 1–2 minutes, until the liquid evaporates and the chard is soft. Stir in the drained quinoa, roasted vegetables and half the parsley. Squeeze in the juice from the lemon, to taste.

8   To serve, slice the lamb steaks against the grain (see Chef's tip on page 127). Transfer the quinoa mix to serving plates and top with the lamb. Garnish with the toasted almonds and remaining parsley.

# Steak with Parsnip Mash & Tarragon Mushroom Sauce

Serves 2

Requiring less water and energy than many other fruit and vegetables, mushrooms are one of the most sustainable crops out there. In this recipe, we celebrate versatile fungi by using dried porcini mushrooms. They create a rich and earthy sauce that is packed with flavour as well as nutrients.

200g white potatoes (we like Maris Piper, King Edward or early autumn), cut into 2cm chunks

400g parsnips, peeled and roughly chopped

½ beef stock cube

10g dried porcini mushrooms

2 × 150g bavette steaks

2 tbsp olive or rapeseed oil

240g chestnut mushrooms, thinly sliced

1 tsp apple cider vinegar

200ml plant-based cream (we use almond cream)

300g Savoy cabbage, finely sliced

handful of tarragon, leaves stripped and finely chopped

sea salt and black pepper

1   Place the potatoes and parsnips in a saucepan of lightly salted boiling water. Simmer for 10–15 minutes until softened, then drain and return to the pan.

2   Dissolve the stock cube in a jug with 200ml boiling water, add the dried porcini and leave to rehydrate and infuse the liquid. Heat a large frying pan with 1 tablespoon of oil on a medium–high heat. Add the steaks and cook until golden brown. As a guide cook for 3–4 minutes on each side for medium–rare and 5–6 minutes on each side for well done.

3   Remove the steaks from the pan and transfer to a plate to rest. Add the chestnut mushrooms to the same frying pan with 1 tablespoon of oil and turn the heat up to high. Fry for 2–3 minutes, until golden brown, then add the vinegar followed by the porcini and their stock and half the cream. Season with salt and pepper then boil for 5 minutes.

4   Meanwhile, place the cabbage in a saucepan of lightly salted boiling water. Simmer for 5 minutes until softened, then drain. Season with salt and pepper.

5   Add the tarragon to the mushroom sauce. Pour the remaining cream into the drained potatoes and parsnips. Season with salt and pepper then mash until smooth. Scoop the mash on to serving plates and place the cabbage and steaks next to it. Pour the sauce over the steaks and serve.

# Spiced Roast Beef with Cumin & Carrot Purée

Serves 2

Colourful and nutritious, there is a reason carrots are such a staple vegetable in the UK. Rich in vitamin A and beta-carotene, we've combined their naturally sweet flavour with cumin seeds, to create a standout accompaniment to the lightly spiced steak.

500g white potatoes (we like Maris Piper, King Edward or early autumn), cut into 3cm chunks

3 banana shallots, peeled and halved lengthways

1 tbsp olive or rapeseed oil

60g kale, leaves stripped from their stalks and roughly chopped

3 carrots, roughly diced

2 tsp cumin seeds

20g flaked almonds

2 × 150g flat-iron steaks

1 tbsp mild curry powder

1 tsp cornflour

½ beef stock cube

sea salt and black pepper

15g pea shoots, to garnish

1   Preheat the oven to 240°C/220°C fan/gas 9. Line a large roasting tin with baking paper.

2   Put the potatoes and shallot into the lined tray, drizzle over ½ tablespoon of oil, then season with salt and pepper. Roast for 25–30 minutes, until soft and golden brown. Add the kale to the tray for the last 5–6 minutes of the cooking time.

3   Bring a small saucepan half-filled with salted water to the boil and add the carrots. Add half the cumin seeds and boil for 20 minutes, until very soft, then drain, reserving 50ml of the cooking liquid. Transfer the carrots and reserved liquid to a blender and blend until smooth, adding a little extra water if necessary.

4   Heat a large frying pan on a medium–high heat. Toast the almonds for 2–3 minutes, turning regularly, until golden. Remove from the pan and set aside then put the pan back on the heat and turn the heat up to high.

5   Add ½ tablespoon of oil to the frying pan, then add the steaks. Season with salt and cook until golden brown on each side. As a guide cook for 3–4 minutes on each side for medium–rare and 5–6 minutes on each side for well done. Dust half the curry powder over the steaks, cook for a final 30 seconds, then remove from the pan and transfer to a plate to rest while you make the gravy.

6   To make the gravy, dissolve the cornflour in a jug with 50ml cold water, then add the stock cube and top up with 250ml boiling water. Add the remaining curry powder and cumin seeds to the pan used for the steak. Toast for 30 seconds, add the stock and cornflour mix and boil for 3–4 minutes, until thickened.

7   To serve, slice the steaks against the grain (see Chef's tip on page 127). Divide the carrot purée between plates, top with the steaks and serve the potatoes, shallots and kale on the side. Garnish with the pea shoots and almonds. Pour over the gravy or serve it in a jug alongside.

# Orange & Pistachio Buckwheat Pudding with Roasted Plums

Serves 2

As soon as plums are ripe, they don't last very long. In this recipe, we suggest using those slightly softer fruits to create an impressive but easy dessert. When cooked, plums naturally create delicious jammy juices; add a spritz of orange juice for zing and you've got yourself the perfect topper to any creamy dessert.

120g buckwheat

1 tsp ground cinnamon

2 tsp vanilla extract

1 × 400ml tin of coconut milk

600ml plant-based milk (we use almond milk)

6 tbsp maple syrup

2 plums, halved and stoned

2 star anise

grated zest and juice of 1 orange

15g pistachio nuts, roughly chopped

sea salt

1   Preheat the oven to 230°C/210°C fan/gas 8.

2   Heat a medium saucepan on a medium heat and add the buckwheat. Toast for 2–3 minutes then add the cinnamon, vanilla, coconut milk, plant-based milk, 4 tablespoons of the maple syrup and a pinch of salt. Simmer for 30–35 minutes, stirring occasionally, until the buckwheat is soft and the sauce is creamy and thick. Add a splash more plant milk if the sauce thickens too much before the buckwheat has cooked.

3   Place the plums cut-side down in a small 15 × 20cm baking dish with the remaining 2 tablespoons of maple syrup and the star anise, then add the orange juice. Roast for 15–20 minutes, until the plums are soft and the sauce has thickened to a syrup. If you notice the liquid burning around the edges of the baking dish before the plums are soft, add a little more water.

4   Serve the buckwheat pudding in bowls topped with the roasted plums, pistachios and orange zest.

# Winter

Often we're sheltering from the harsh weather conditions our island faces at this time of the year, but time indoors means that winter brings the opportunity to spend more time in the kitchen.

It's time to celebrate brassicas and root veg, such as Brussels sprouts and parsnips. Pumpkins are often believed to be best saved for carving at Hallowe'en, but there are so many different shapes, sizes and colours of pumpkins, and squash, we'd encourage you to give the different varieties a try.

We champion lots of the classic winter vegetables in this chapter, including cabbages, kale and swede, but we think some of the lesser known ingredients are the most interesting. With a relatively short season that can easily be missed, now is the time to make the most of Jerusalem artichokes – try them in the hearty stew on page 178. Salsify is another really delicious root vegetable that has an almost oyster-like flavour when cooked. It can be slightly harder to find – your best bet will be your local farmers' market, greengrocer or an online retailer.

This season may be seem the longest and, for some, the hardest, but the rich variety of contrasting textures and flavours offered by the vegetables and fruit at this time of year can offer comfort. And as we near the end of winter and the first signs of spring start to emerge as the fields come to life again, we become excited by the prospect of spending more time in the great outdoors, foraging in the fields or in local farmers' markets for the new ingredients that become available.

# Curried Parsnip, Lentil, Pear & Walnut Salad

### Serves 2

200g parsnips, peeled and cut lengthways into 3cm wedges

about 2 tbsp olive or rapeseed oil

1 tbsp curry powder

40g walnuts

40g quinoa

80g coconut yoghurt

1 lemon

2 banana shallots, finely sliced

1 × 400g tin of lentils, drained and rinsed

1 pear, cored, cut into quarters lengthways and thinly sliced

handful of mint, leaves picked and finely chopped

1 pomegranate, cut in half, seeds removed (see Chef's tip)

20g rocket

sea salt and black pepper

### Chef's tip

To remove the pomegranate seeds easily, halve the fruit and hold one half, cut-side down, over a large bowl. Using a wooden spoon, give the pomegranate a good strong tap, hitting it until all the seeds have fallen out. Repeat with the other half, then pick out any white membrane that may have fallen out with the seeds. If you have more seeds than you would like to use, they can easily be stored in the freezer for up to 3 months.

A sweet fruit that comes in thousands of varieties, pears are in season between September and January. Not only an ingredient for desserts, pears can also be used in savoury cooking, such as in this crunchy salad. Brightened with curry spice, their natural sweetness is complemented by bitter leaves and savoury lentils in the veg-packed dish.

1   Preheat the oven to 220°C/200°C fan/gas 7. Line a baking tray with baking paper.

2   Put the parsnips into the lined tray and drizzle with 2 teaspoons of oil. Sprinkle over half the curry powder and season with salt and pepper. Toss to coat, then roast for 15–20 minutes, until golden and cooked through. Towards the end of their cooking time, add the walnuts to a separate tray and cook for 5 minutes.

3   Add the quinoa to a small saucepan of salted boiling water and boil for 13–14 minutes, until cooked, then drain.

4   Put the yoghurt into a bowl, and grate in the zest from the lemon. Cut the lemon in half and add the juice from half along with ½ tablespoon of cold water to make a drizzling consistency. Season with a pinch of salt.

5   Heat a large, deep frying pan with 1 tablespoon of oil on a medium heat and cook the shallot for 6–8 minutes, stirring occasionally, until soft and golden. Season with a pinch of salt.

6   Once the shallot is soft and golden, stir in the remaining curry powder and cook for 30 seconds. Stir the lentils into the pan, followed by the cooked quinoa, parsnip, pear, mint, a squeeze of lemon juice, to taste, and half the pomegranate seeds. Season with salt and pepper.

7   Mix together well, then gently stir though the rocket. Transfer to plates and sprinkle over the walnuts and remaining pomegranate. Drizzle over the lemon yoghurt.

# Thyme & Garlic-Roasted Artichokes with Creamy Cannellini Beans

Serves 2

Hearty Jerusalem artichokes are the star of this creamy bean stew. Roasted with earthy thyme and plenty of garlic, they become pockets of crispy-skinned deliciousness. Rich in iron, potassium and vitamin B1, the Jerusalem artichoke is a vegetable we should all be paying a little more attention to during its short season, running from late autumn through to early spring.

250g Jerusalem artichokes

4 garlic cloves, finely chopped

small handful of thyme, leaves stripped and roughly chopped

1 tbsp olive or rapeseed oil

1 banana shallot, finely chopped

1 leek, trimmed and sliced into 1cm half-moons

2 tbsp nutritional yeast

2 tbsp sundried tomato paste

80g kale, leaves stripped from their stalks and sliced

½ vegetable stock cube

200ml almond cream

1 × 400g tin of cannellini beans, drained and rinsed

2 tbsp cashew butter

10g hazelnuts, roughly chopped

1 lemon

sea salt and black pepper

1   Preheat the oven to 240°C/220°C fan/gas 9. Line a baking tray with baking paper.

2   Scrub the artichokes lightly with a scourer (see Chef's Tip), being sure to remove any grit. Halve the small ones and quarter the bigger ones. Place the artichokes, half the garlic and half the thyme in the lined tray and toss with ½ tablespoon of oil and some salt and pepper. Roast for 25–30 minutes, until the artichokes are soft and golden.

3   Heat a large saucepan with ½ tablespoon of oil on a medium heat. Add the shallot, leek and remaining garlic and thyme. Season with salt and cook for 6–7 minutes until soft. Add the nutritional yeast, tomato paste, half the kale and stir to combine.

4   Dissolve the stock cube in a jug with 250ml boiling water. Add the stock, almond cream, beans and cashew butter to the pan and simmer for 6–8 minutes, stirring regularly, until the liquid has thickened. Add more water if necessary during the cooking to ensure a loose risotto consistency is achieved. Season generously with salt.

5   Meanwhile, place the hazelnuts in a small bowl and toss with the remaining kale, cut the lemon in half and add a good squeeze of lemon juice and a pinch of salt.

6   Serve the beans in bowls, topped with the kale and roasted artichokes. Serve the remaining lemon as wedges.

## Chef's tip

Like many root vegetables, Jerusalem artichokes need a bit of extra prep time to remove all the grit and soil attached to their rough skin. Using a scourer will really help with this.

# Roasted Root Veg Salad with Sage & Walnut Yoghurt Dressing

Serves 2

Kale is one of the most nutrient-dense foods on the planet: 100g of raw kale contains just 49 calories, while still providing 4g of protein, 5g of fibre and significant amounts of iron, calcium and magnesium. While delicious eaten raw, in this recipe we roast the leaves, giving the roasted vegetable salad texture and a wintery emerald green hue. Have some kale leftover? The crisp leaves also make a great snack! Just allow them to cool, then store them in an airtight container for up to 3 days.

1 red onion

150g sweet potato, skin on, cut into thin wedges

200g beetroot, trimmed and cut into 6 wedges

2 tbsp olive or rapeseed oil

3 tbsp red wine vinegar

20g walnuts, roughly chopped

handful of sage, leaves stripped and finely chopped

80g almond yoghurt

40g kale, leaves stripped from their stalks and roughly chopped

80g grapes, cut in half

sea salt and black pepper

1   Preheat the oven to 220°C/200°C fan/gas 7. Line a baking tray with baking paper.

2   Finely slice one half of the onion and cut the rest into wedges. Place the sweet potato, beetroot and onion wedges into the lined tray, drizzle with ½ tablespoon of oil then season with salt and pepper. Roast for 20 minutes, until the veg is soft and the potatoes are golden brown.

3   Meanwhile, place the sliced onion in a small bowl and mix with the red wine vinegar and a pinch of salt. Mix and set aside to pickle.

4   Heat a small frying pan with ½ teaspoon of oil on a medium heat. Toast the walnuts for 2–3 minutes, tossing regularly, until they begin to brown. Stir in the sage, cook for 10 seconds, then remove from the heat and stir in the yoghurt, a splash of water and a pinch of salt.

5   After 20 minutes of roasting, add the kale to the tray with the roasted vegetables. Drizzle with 1 teaspoon of oil and season with a pinch of salt. Roast for a further 5–8 minutes, until the kale is golden and crisp. Remove from the oven.

6   Finally, stir the grapes and pickled onion into the roasted vegetables. Transfer to serving plates and spoon over the walnut and sage yoghurt.

# Breaded Mushroom with Roast Potatoes & Red Cabbage

**Serves 2**

Braised red cabbage is the sneaky star of this dish. We simmer it with apple, maple syrup and a splash of vinegar until soft, to tenderise the cabbage and create a dish bursting with balanced flavour. Rich in antioxidants, red cabbage has been proven to fight inflammation and support heart health.

300g baby white potatoes, sliced lengthways into thirds

2 tbsp olive or rapeseed oil

35g chickpea flour

½ tbsp dried oregano

4 tbsp ground almonds

2 Portobello mushrooms, stalks removed

handful of chives, finely chopped

100g almond yoghurt

½ tbsp wholegrain mustard

200g red cabbage, finely sliced

1 eating apple, cored and coarsely grated

2 tbsp red wine vinegar

1 tbsp maple syrup

sea salt and black pepper

 Chef's tip

A versatile winter vegetable, don't worry if you have any red cabbage left over; there is so much you can do with it! Enjoy it crunchy in a refreshing coleslaw or shred it and roast it with spices for 15–20 minutes as a warming side. Adding vinegar to any preparation helps retain the cabbage's bright purple hue and adds some zing.

1   Preheat the oven to 220°C/200°C fan/gas 7. Line two baking trays with baking paper.

2   Place the potatoes in one of the lined trays, drizzle with 1 teaspoon of oil and season with salt and pepper. Set aside.

3   In a small bowl, mix the chickpea flour with 4 tablespoons of water to make a smooth batter. In another small bowl, mix the oregano with the ground almonds and season generously with salt.

4   Place the mushrooms in the other lined tray, gill sides up, then spoon the chickpea batter over the top of each one to cover evenly. Divide the herby almond crumb between the mushrooms, gently pressing it into the batter. Drizzle 2 teaspoons of oil over the top, then put both trays in the oven for 20–25 minutes, until the potatoes and mushrooms are soft and golden.

5   Meanwhile, place the chives in a small bowl. Add the almond yoghurt and mustard and season with a pinch of salt. Mix well and set aside.

6   Heat 1 tablespoon of oil in a large frying pan on a medium–high heat. Add the cabbage, apple and vinegar to the pan, along with 50ml water and a good pinch of salt and pepper. Cook, stirring regularly, for 5 minutes until the cabbage is starting to soften, then stir in the maple syrup and continue to cook for 5 more minutes, until softened.

7   Once ready, serve the mushrooms with the cabbage and roasted potatoes on the side. Dollop a spoonful of chive yoghurt on top.

# Creamy Pumpkin & Wild Mushroom Penne Bake

Serves 2

This macaroni-cheese-inspired dish is rich, creamy and completely plant-based. By puréeing roasted squash and combining it with miso, nutritional yeast and cashew cream, we've created a delicious cheesy-flavoured sauce with the texture of a béchamel, which also contributes to your five-a-day. Mixed with pasta and topped with crunchy seeds, you're on to a winter winner.

1 × 500–700g eating pumpkin (we like Ironbark or Delica) or butternut squash, peeled and cut into 2cm cubes (seeds reserved)

2 garlic cloves, unpeeled

2½ tbsp olive or rapeseed oil

120g brown rice penne

½ vegetable stock cube

200g wild mushrooms

80g spinach

10g thyme, leaves stripped and finely chopped

2 tbsp nutritional yeast

200ml cashew cream

2 tbsp white miso

1 tbsp Dijon mustard

1 tsp smoked paprika

1 tbsp ground almonds

sea salt and black pepper

1   Preheat the oven to 220°C/200°C fan/gas 7. Line a baking tray with baking paper.

2   Place the pumpkin and garlic cloves on the lined tray, drizzle with 1 tablespoon of oil and season with salt and pepper. Roast for 25–30 minutes, until soft and golden.

3   Cook the penne in a pan of salted boiling water for 7–8 minutes or according to the instructions on the pack, then drain, run under cold water and drain again.

4   Meanwhile, wash the pumpkin seeds under cold water. Pat them dry and set aside. Dissolve the stock cube in a jug with 100ml boiling water.

5   Roughly chop any larger mushrooms. Heat a large frying pan with 1 tablespoon of oil and cook the mushrooms for 3–4 minutes until starting to soften. Stir in the spinach and half the thyme and cook for 1–2 minutes more, until the spinach has wilted. Season to taste with salt and pepper.

6   Once cooked, carefully peel the garlic cloves and place in a blender along with the roasted pumpkin, nutritional yeast, cashew cream, miso, mustard and smoked paprika. Add 50ml of the stock and blend until smooth. Add the remaining 50ml if needed to create a smooth purée with the consistency of a thick soup. Season with salt and pepper. Preheat the grill to high.

7   Return the pasta to its pan and stir in the mushrooms, spinach and butternut squash purée.

8   Toss to coat everything well, then transfer to a small baking dish. Combine the ground almonds, reserved pumpkin seeds and remaining thyme in a small bowl. Mix with ½ tablespoon of oil and season with a pinch of salt. Sprinkle over the creamy penne, then place under the grill for 8–10 minutes, until golden and bubbling.

# Winter Falafel & Crispy Sprout Protein Bowl

Serves 2

We have seasonalised this gym-goer's favourite with Brussels sprouts. Roasted with maple syrup until crisp, then paired with pickled onions, we dare you not to love them in this recipe. Served alongside protein-packed falafel and quinoa, this bowl is designed to leave you full and satisfied.

1 red onion

grated zest and juice of 1 lemon

80g tricolour quinoa

150g Brussels sprouts

3½ tbsp olive or rapeseed oil

½ tbsp maple syrup

1 × 400g tin of chickpeas, drained and rinsed

2 tbsp chickpea flour

1 tbsp ground cumin

2 tsp ground turmeric

½ tsp chilli flakes

10g mint, leaves picked and finely chopped

20g flat-leaf parsley, finely chopped

20g coriander, finely chopped

1 avocado

80g almond yoghurt

1 carrot, cut into thin matchsticks or coarsely grated

2 tsp white sesame seeds

sea salt and black pepper

1   Preheat the oven to 220°C/200°C fan/gas 7. Line a baking tray with baking paper.

2   Finely chop half the onion and finely slice the other half. Place the sliced onion in a small bowl and mix with half the lemon juice and a pinch of salt. Mix well, then set aside.

3   Meanwhile, add the quinoa to a large saucepan of salted boiling water and boil for 13–14 minutes, until cooked, then drain and allow to cool.

4   Trim the root from the sprouts, then separate the leaves. Toss the leaves with 1½ teaspoons of oil, the maple syrup and a pinch of salt and pepper. Transfer to the lined tray and roast for 5 minutes, until beginning to char, then remove from the oven.

5   Dry the chickpeas thoroughly with a clean tea towel and transfer to a large mixing bowl. Add the chickpea flour, cumin, turmeric, chilli flakes, to taste, chopped onion and half of each herb. Season well with salt and pepper, then mash thoroughly, using your hands.

6   Bring the chickpea mixture together, then shape into 8 equal-sized patties. Heat 3 tablespoons of oil in a large frying pan on a medium heat and fry the patties for 3–4 minutes on each side, until golden. Transfer to the tray of sprout leaves and bake in the oven for 8–10 minutes, until the falafels are cooked through, and the Brussels sprouts are charred and crispy.

7   Meanwhile, thinly slice the avocado. Place the remaining mint in a small bowl with the yoghurt and the remaining lemon juice. Season with salt and pepper. Once cooled, season the quinoa with a pinch of salt and lemon zest, to taste, then stir in the remaining parsley and coriander.

8   To serve, place the falafels into serving bowls with the crispy sprouts, herby quinoa, avocado, carrot and pickled onion alongside. Add a good spoonful of the minty yoghurt on top, and sprinkle over the sesame seeds.

# Maple & Ginger Glazed Roast Swede with a Peanut & Lime Dressing

Serves 2

A wonderful source of vitamin C, swede is often overlooked in favour of other root vegetables like parsnips and potatoes. However, they're a great low-carb alternative for those who want to keep their glycaemic index in check. In season from October to February, swede can be prepared in a variety of ways to celebrate its natural sweetness — Asian flavours pair well with it, so here we've coated it in peanut butter, tamari and maple syrup to make it shine.

1 swede (400–600g), peeled and cut into 2cm chunks

30g smooth peanut butter

3 tbsp tamari

juice of 1 lime

6 tbsp maple syrup

1 tbsp white sesame seeds

100g brown rice noodles

2 tbsp olive or rapeseed oil

2cm ginger, finely chopped

80g cavolo nero, leaves stripped from their stalk and roughly chopped

sea salt

1 red chilli, finely sliced (remove the seeds for less heat), to garnish (optional)

10g mustard cress, to garnish

1 Place the swede in a saucepan of salted boiling water. Simmer for 15–17 minutes, until just soft, then drain.

2 To make the dressing, in a small bowl combine the peanut butter, tamari, lime juice, half the maple syrup and the sesame seeds. Add a splash of water and stir to get a drizzling consistency.

3 Cook the noodles in salted boiling water for 3–4 minutes or according to the instructions on the pack, gently separating them with a fork, then drain and rinse well.

4 Heat a medium frying pan with the oil on a medium–high heat. Add the drained swede and fry for 2–3 minutes, then add the ginger and pour in the remaining maple syrup. Fry for another 3–4 minutes, until the maple syrup begins to go sticky, then add the cavolo nero, stir and cook for a final 1–2 minutes until it wilts.

5 In a large bowl toss the swede, cavolo nero, noodles and dressing. Season with salt then transfer to serving plates and garnish with the chilli, if using, and the mustard cress.

# Cod with Roasted Salsify & Cauliflower Risotto with Hazelnut Pesto

Serves 2

Salsify is a root veg with a delicate and slightly sweet flavour, in season between October and January. This risotto combines grated cauliflower with rice in a lower-carbohydrate version of an indulgent classic. Topped with a hazelnut pesto, this easy meal will not fail to impress.

80g salsify, peeled, trimmed and cut into 4cm lengths

4 tbsp olive oil

50g brown rice

1 small head of cauliflower

2 shallots, finely diced

small handful of thyme sprigs, leaves stripped and finely chopped

3 garlic cloves, finely chopped or crushed

50ml white wine (optional)

2 × 150g cod fillets, with skin

1 vegetable stock cube

100ml plant-based cream (we use cashew cream)

2 tbsp nutritional yeast

20g hazelnuts, finely chopped

10g flat-leaf parsley, finely chopped

1 lemon, halved

sea salt and black pepper

1   Preheat the oven to 220°C/200°C fan/gas 7. Line a baking tray with baking paper.

2   Place the salsify to one side of the lined tray. Mix with 1 tablespoon of oil and some salt and pepper. Roast in the oven for 15 minutes.

3   Meanwhile, add the rice to a large saucepan of salted boiling water and boil for 25–30 minutes, until cooked, then drain.

4   Remove the leaves from the cauliflower and set to one side. Cut the cauliflower head into quarters and coarsely grate into a rice consistency (including the stalk). You can also do this in a food processor using a fine grater blade if you have one.

5   Heat a medium frying pan with 1 teaspoon of oil on a medium heat. Add the grated cauliflower, shallot, thyme and three quarters of the garlic. Cook for 5–7 minutes, stirring occasionally, until everything is starting to soften. Pour in the wine, if using, and bubble until almost completely evaporated.

6   After the salsify has roasted for 15 minutes, add the cauliflower leaves and cod, skin-side up, to the tray. Drizzle over 2 teaspoons of oil and season with salt and pepper. Roast for another 10–15 minutes, until the fish is cooked.

7   Meanwhile, dissolve half the stock cube in a jug with 100ml boiling water and add to the frying pan with the cauliflower, along with the cashew cream and nutritional yeast, mix, bring to the boil, then lower the heat and simmer until reduced by half.

8   For the pesto, add the hazelnuts, parsley, remaining garlic and juice from half the lemon to a bowl with 2 tablespoons of olive oil. Season.

9   Stir the drained rice into the cauliflower cream and cook for another 5 minutes, until the sauce is thick and coating the rice. Add a splash of water if it looks dry. Season to taste with a squeeze of lemon juice and salt and pepper. Serve the cauli-rice risotto with the cod, salsify and cauliflower leaves on top. Drizzle over the hazelnut pesto and garnish with the remaining lemon, cut into slices.

 Chef's tip

You know your fish is cooked when it flakes easily with a fork and turns completely white, losing its transparent or raw appearance.

# Sea Bass with Sage Romesco & Charred Sprouts

Serves 2

We are Brussels sprout lovers here at Mindful Chef, and as they come with a variety of health benefits, we think you should be too. Like many brassicas, they are high in fibre, helping to stabilise blood sugar levels and support gut health. Here, we maximise their flavour by roasting them and serving them on top of a punchy homemade romesco sauce.

3 red peppers, deseeded and cut into 2cm squares

about 3 tbsp olive or rapeseed oil

20g flaked almonds

40g kale, leaves stripped from their stalks and roughly chopped

300g baby white potatoes, quartered lengthways

1 leek, trimmed and quartered lengthways, then cut into 4cm lengths

100g Brussels sprouts, cut in half

2 × 120g sea bass fillets, with skin

1 lemon

handful of sage, leaves picked

2 garlic cloves

1 tsp smoked paprika

1 tbsp extra virgin olive oil

sea salt and black pepper

1  Preheat the oven to 240°C/220°C fan/gas 9. Line a baking tray with baking paper.

2  Place the pepper on the lined tray, drizzle over 1 tablespoon of oil and season with salt and pepper. Roast for 25 minutes, until soft and beginning to blacken in places. Around 5 minutes before the pepper is ready, push it to one side of the tray. Add the kale to the other side with 1 teaspoon of oil and a pinch of salt. Mix the almonds with the peppers and return to the oven for the final 5 minutes.

3  Place the potatoes in a saucepan of salted boiling water. Simmer for 10–12 minutes, until tender, then drain.

4  Heat a large frying pan with 2 teaspoons of oil over a high heat. Add the Brussels sprouts, season with salt and cook for 4–5 minutes, turning occasionally, until blackening in places. Add the leek and potatoes to the pan and continue to cook for 4–5 minutes, until beginning to blacken in places.

5  While the vegetables are charring, season the sea bass with salt. Heat a medium non-stick frying pan with 1 tablespoon of oil on a high heat, then add the fillets, skin-side down, and cook for 3–4 minutes, until golden underneath. Flip and fry for a further 2–3 minutes, until cooked. Squeeze in a little lemon juice and remove from the heat.

6  To make the romesco sauce, transfer the peppers and almonds to a chopping board with half the sage, the garlic, paprika and extra virgin olive oil and a pinch of sea salt. Finely chop together making a rough paste, then place in a bowl.

7  Add the remaining sage to the charred vegetables and finish with a squeeze of lemon juice, to taste, then remove from the heat.To serve, spoon the romesco sauce into the centre of serving plates and spread. Arrange the potatoes and vegetables on top, then add the sea bass. Garnish with the crispy kale.

# Black Garlic Chicken with Celeriac Fondant & Roasted Veg

Serves 2

Celeriac is a knobbly, bulbous root vegetable that is a fantastic, lighter alternative to potatoes. Good for bone health and digestion, celeriac can be enjoyed raw and cooked. Here we slowly roast it in stock, thyme and nutritional yeast, giving time for its firm form to soften and turn smooth and velvety.

400g celeriac, peeled, trimmed and halved to make two 2–3cm discs

2 tbsp olive or rapeseed oil

½ chicken stock cube

handful of thyme sprigs, leaves stripped and finely chopped

1 tbsp nutritional yeast

300g carrots, peeled and cut into batons

2 shallots, cut into quarters

8 black garlic cloves

2 tbsp tomato purée

1 tbsp clear honey

2 × 150g chicken breast fillets

1 tsp cornflour

sea salt and black pepper

handful of pea shoots, to garnish

1   Preheat the oven to 220°C/200°C fan/gas 7. Line a baking tray with baking paper.

2   Heat a large ovenproof frying pan with 1 tablespoon of oil on a medium–high heat. Season the celeriac with salt and fry for 3 minutes on each side or until golden.

3   Dissolve the stock cube in a jug with 350ml boiling water. Pour the stock over the celeriac, then add the thyme and nutritional yeast. Boil for 5 minutes, then transfer the pan to the oven (see Chef's Tip). Bake for 20–25 minutes, until the celeriac is soft.

4   Put the carrots and shallot into the lined tray and drizzle with 2 teaspoons of oil; season with salt and pepper. Roast for 10 minutes.

5   Meanwhile, use the flat of a knife to mash the black garlic into a paste. Mix with the tomato purée, honey and 1 teaspoon of oil in a shallow bowl, then add the chicken and coat it in the mixture. After the carrots have been cooking for 10 minutes, add the chicken to the tray and season with salt and pepper. Roast for 15–20 minutes or until the chicken is cooked through. Check this by inserting a skewer into the thickest part of the meat; the juices should run clear. Cook for longer if necessary.

6   Dissolve the cornflour in 3 tablespoons of water in a small bowl. Transfer the celeriac on to serving plates and return the pan to a medium–high heat. Stir in the cornflour mix then simmer for 1–2 minutes, until thickened (add more water if necessary to get a glossy sauce).

7   Serve the carrots, shallots and chicken with the celeriac. Pour over the sauce and garnish with the pea shoots.

 Chef's tip

If you don't have an ovenproof frying pan, just transfer the celeriac to a small ovenproof dish or roasting tin and continue to follow the recipe.

# Creamy Chicken Pie
# with Chestnut Roasted Broccoli

Serves 2

In season from October through to December, chestnuts are a seasonal favourite in the UK. Although higher in carbohydrate than other nuts, their high water, low oil content means they are also lower in calories. Rich in fibre, they help to regulate blood sugar levels, meaning you stay fuller for longer. Served with broccoli, alongside a creamy apple, leek and chicken pie, we think this recipe is the essence of winter.

½ chicken stock cube

400g large white potatoes, peeled and roughly chopped into 2cm chunks

½ tbsp extra virgin olive oil

1½ tbsp olive or rapeseed oil

300g skinless, boneless chicken thighs, cut into 3cm chunks

1 eating apple, peeled, cored and cut into 1cm chunks

1 leek, thinly sliced

2 garlic cloves, finely chopped or crushed

2 thyme sprigs, leaves stripped and finely chopped

1 tbsp wholegrain mustard

1 tbsp gluten-free flour (we use buckwheat flour)

200ml plant-based cream (we use almond cream)

200g Tenderstem broccoli

100g pre-cooked chestnuts, roughly chopped

sea salt and black pepper

1   Preheat the oven to 220°C/200°C fan/gas 7.

2   Dissolve the stock cube in a jug with 200ml boiling water.

3   Place the potatoes in a saucepan of salted boiling water. Simmer for 18–20 minutes, until soft, then drain. Return the potatoes to the pan and mash with the extra virgin olive oil and some salt and pepper.

4   Heat a large frying pan with 1 tablespoon of the oil on a medium heat. Add the chicken and apple and season with salt and pepper, then cook for 5 minutes, until turning golden brown. Add the leek, along with the garlic and cook for a further 5 minutes.

5   Add the thyme, mustard and flour to the pan, continue to cook for a further minute, stirring, then slowly add the stock and cream. Season with salt and pepper. Simmer for 10–12 minutes, until the sauce is thick.

6   Place the mixture in a 20 × 20cm baking dish and top with the mash. Bake for 15 minutes, until bubbling.

7   While the pie is baking, heat a frying pan with ½ tablespoon of oil on a medium–high heat and cook the broccoli for 4–5 minutes, stirring occasionally, until deep golden brown. Add the chestnuts and 3 tablespoons of water and continue to cook for 2–3 minutes until the broccoli is just soft. Serve the pie with the chestnut roasted broccoli.

# Pork, Apple & Tarragon Tray Bake

Serves 2

This is an impressive dish that's deceptively easy to make. One of the most widely grown fruits, apples are a staple in many households. They make a wonderful snack, but have you ever tried pairing them with pork. They're a perfect match. Adding apples to savoury dishes also brings out their natural tartness.

2 banana shallots, halved lengthways

2 eating apples, cored and cut into wedges

1 × 400–600g butternut squash, peeled, seeds removed, flesh cut into 2cm cubes

180g Tenderstem broccoli

20g walnuts

2 tbsp wholegrain mustard

2 tbsp clear honey

4 tsp olive or rapeseed oil

2 × 170g pork loins

handful of tarragon, leaves stripped and finely chopped

sea salt and black pepper

1   Preheat the oven to 220°C/200°C fan/gas 7. Line a large roasting tin with baking paper.

2   Put the shallot, apples, squash, broccoli and walnuts into the lined tin.

3   In a bowl, combine the mustard, honey and 2 teaspoons of oil, drizzle over the tray of vegetables and season everything with salt and pepper, then toss to coat. Roast for 20–25 minutes, until the veg is soft and golden brown.

4   About 10 minutes before the vegetables are ready, heat a medium frying pan with 2 teaspoons of oil on a high heat. Add the pork and fry for 2–3 minutes on each side, until deep golden brown. Season with salt and pepper, then once the veg is done, add the pork to the tray. Drizzle over any juices from the pan and roast for a final 5 minutes.

5   Stir the tarragon through the vegetables, then serve the veg topped with the pork.

# Spiced Venison Koftas with Nutty Sage Rice

Serves 2

Minced venison comes from the shoulder or flank of a deer and is leaner and higher in protein than most other forms of red meat. As the UK has a thriving deer population, it needs to be managed to ensure the animals and their environment remain healthy, making it arguably one of the most sustainable and ethical sources of meat available. Give it a go in this recipe, where we balance its naturally rich and earthy flavour with clementine zest, cinnamon and allspice.

80g brown rice

300g minced venison

grated zest of 2 clementines

3 garlic cloves, finely chopped or crushed

½ tsp ground cinnamon

½ tsp allspice

1 tbsp olive or rapeseed oil

25g clear honey

200g passata

80g kale, leaves stripped from their stalks and roughly chopped

80g baby spinach, finely chopped

5g sage, leaves picked and roughly chopped

20g raisins

20g unsalted pistachio nuts, roughly chopped

sea salt and black pepper

1   Preheat the oven to 240°C/220°C fan/gas 9. Line a baking tray with baking paper.

2   Add the rice to a large saucepan of salted boiling water and boil for 25–30 minutes, until cooked, then drain and return it to the pan.

3   In a bowl, combine the venison with the clementine zest, garlic, half the cinnamon and half the allspice. Season with salt and pepper. With wet hands, shape the mix into 4 sausage-shaped koftas.

4   Heat a medium, ovenproof frying pan with ½ tablespoon of oil on a medium–high heat. Cook the koftas for 3–4 minutes, turning occasionally, until golden brown all over. Add the honey and cook for 2–3 minutes, stirring frequently, until the honey turns dark brown. Stir in the passata and transfer to the oven. Bake for 10–12 minutes, until the sauce reduces slightly and the meat is no longer pink in the middle.

5   Meanwhile, put the kale into the lined tray and toss with ½ tablespoon of oil and some salt and pepper. Roast for 4–5 minutes, until crisp.

6   Add the spinach and sage to the cooked rice along with the raisins and remaining spices. Cut one of the clementines in half and squeeze in the juice, to taste. Peel and add the segments from the other clementine to the rice. Mix well.

7   Spread the tomato sauce on to serving plates and top with the rice mix. Add the koftas and scatter over the kale and pistachios.

# Swedish Meatballs with Dill & Cranberries

Serves 2

Usually made with lingonberries, we've used cranberries to lower the sugar content and up the fibre in this traditional Swedish dish. Paired with pork meatballs and mashed potato, this is a healthy comforting winter meal.

300g baby white potatoes

4 carrots, peeled and sliced

80g spinach

2 tsp cornflour

½ beef stock cube

300g minced pork

2 tbsp olive oil

1 banana shallot, finely diced

½ tsp ground allspice

½ tsp ground nutmeg

3 tbsp Cranberry Sauce (see recipe on page 191)

80g almond yoghurt

handful of dill, finely chopped, plus a few sprigs to garnish

sea salt and black pepper

1  Place the potatoes in a saucepan of salted boiling water. Simmer for 10 minutes, then add the carrots and simmer for another 1–15 minutes until soft. Add the spinach for the final 1 minute, then drain.

2  Dissolve the cornflour in a jug with 3 tablespoons of water then add the stock cube and top up with 200ml boiling water.

3  Roll the minced pork into 10 small meatballs. Heat a medium frying pan with 1 tablespoon of oil on a medium–high heat and fry the meatballs for 2–3 minutes, until golden brown in places. Add the shallot along with the allspice and nutmeg. Fry for another 2 minutes, then season with salt and pepper. Add the stock and 1 tablespoon of the cranberry sauce then simmer for 10 minutes.

4  Add the yoghurt to the sauce with half of the chopped dill. Cook for a final minute then remove from the heat. Toss the drained vegetables with 1 tablespoon of olive oil, half of the remaining dill and a pinch of salt and pepper.

5  Serve the meatballs in the sauce, alongside the vegetables. Divide the remaining cranberry sauce between the plates and garnish with the dill sprigs.

# Vegan Spiced Pear Sticky Date Pudding with Coconut Caramel Sauce

## Serves 6

100g pitted dates, chopped

1 tbsp ground flaxseed

1 pear, cored and chopped into 1cm pieces

100g ground almonds

1 tsp ground ginger

½ tsp mixed spice

½ tsp ground cinnamon

½ tsp bicarbonate of soda

½ tsp baking powder

55ml vegetable oil

55g coconut sugar

50ml plant-based milk (we use almond)

### FOR THE COCONUT CARAMEL SAUCE

200ml tinned coconut milk

40g coconut sugar

½ tsp vanilla extract

pinch of sea salt

## Chef's tip

You can use up the other half of the tinned coconut milk in a variety of sweet and savoury recipes. Simply add it to your favourite curry recipe (see page 79 for our Chicken Curry with Spiced Carrot Salad). Alternatively, use it instead of coconut cream in the Roasted Sweetheart Cabbage with Chickpea Madras and Chilli Cashews recipe on page 76.

Sticky toffee pudding is all we want in December, so here's a twist on the classic. Using plant-based ingredients to create this rich, sweet dessert, this version also stars British pears, baked until soft and delicious.

1  Preheat the oven to 180°C/160°C fan/gas 4.

2  In a small bowl, soak the dates in 60ml boiling water for 5 minutes. Put the flaxseed in a small bowl and mix in 2½ tablespoons of water, then set aside for 5 minutes, until thickened.

3  Meanwhile, divide the pear between six 5 × 9cm ramekins.

4  Mix the ground almonds with the spices, bicarbonate of soda and baking power in a medium mixing bowl.

5  In a large mixing bowl, whisk the oil with the coconut sugar.

6  Blend the dates, along with their soaking water, into a smooth paste using a blender, then whisk the date paste and flaxseed mixture into the oil and sugar. Gently fold the ground almond mixture into the bowl using a wooden spoon, then mix in the plant-based milk, until a smooth batter forms.

7  Pour the batter into the ramekins, leaving a 1cm gap at the top. Put the ramekins on to a baking tray, transfer to the oven and bake for 35–45 minutes, until the top is golden and firm to the touch.

8  Meanwhile, make the coconut caramel sauce. Put the coconut milk and coconut sugar into a small saucepan. Slowly bring to the boil, stirring to dissolve the sugar, then reduce the heat to low and simmer for 20–25 minutes, until thickened. Once thickened, stir in the vanilla extract and add the salt.

9  Serve the sticky date pudding warm from the oven with the caramel sauce poured on top. If you have any in the fridge, this is fantastic with a dollop of natural plant-based yoghurt dolloped on top too!

# Baked Apples with Maple Custard

Serves 4

Who said dessert had to be unhealthy? Our take on baked apples celebrates the natural sweetness of the fruit to create a truly delicious after-dinner treat. Packed with oats, nuts, dried fruit and plenty of warm spices, this recipe is also full of vitamins, fibre and protein. Think like us and turn this dish into the ultimate winter breakfast if you have any left over.

### FOR THE BAKED APPLES

4 eating apples (we like Braeburn or Cripps Pink)

50g mixed dried fruit (raisins, dried cranberries, sultanas etc.)

25g nuts (we like pecans but almonds and walnuts work well), roughly chopped

25g gluten-free oats

20g coconut sugar

30g coconut oil, melted

4 tsp maple syrup

½ tsp ground cinnamon

½ tsp ground nutmeg

1 orange, zest grated, halved

### FOR THE MAPLE CUSTARD

2 tbsp cornflour

250ml plant-based milk (we use oat milk)

250ml vegan cream (we use oat cream)

3 tbsp maple syrup or to taste

1 tsp vanilla extract

pinch of ground turmeric

1 Preheat the oven to 180°C/160° fan/gas 4.

2 Core the apples using a corer or small knife, then score a line around the middle of each one (horizontally), slicing just through the skin.

3 Put all the remaining ingredients for the baked apples into a large mixing bowl, using only the zest from the orange at this point (the juice will be added later). Stir well to combine, then fill the core of each apple with the dried fruit mix. Place the apples in a small baking dish, the more snug the better.

4 Squeeze the juice from the orange into a measuring jug, then add enough water to bring it up to 150ml of liquid. Pour into the dish with the apples and bake in the oven for 30–35 minutes, until the apples are soft.

5 While the apples are baking, make the custard. Place the cornflour in a small saucepan and add a splash of the milk. Using a whisk or wooden spoon, mix to make a smooth paste, then slowly stir in the remaining milk, followed by the cream, maple syrup and vanilla extract. Add the turmeric and place the pan over a medium–low heat. Stirring continuously, bring the custard up to a simmer and continue to stir until thickened to your desired consistency. Season to taste with a drop more maple or vanilla, if desired.

6 Serve the baked apples immediately and spoon the custard on top.

## Chef's tip

The baked apples and custard can be refrigerated for up to 3 days. To reheat, return the apples to an ovenproof dish, cover with a flat baking tray or greaseproof paper and place in an oven set to 180°C/160°C fan/gas 4 for 10–15 minutes or until warmed through. Place any leftover custard in a small saucepan, add a splash of plant-based milk to loosen, then warm through on a medium heat.

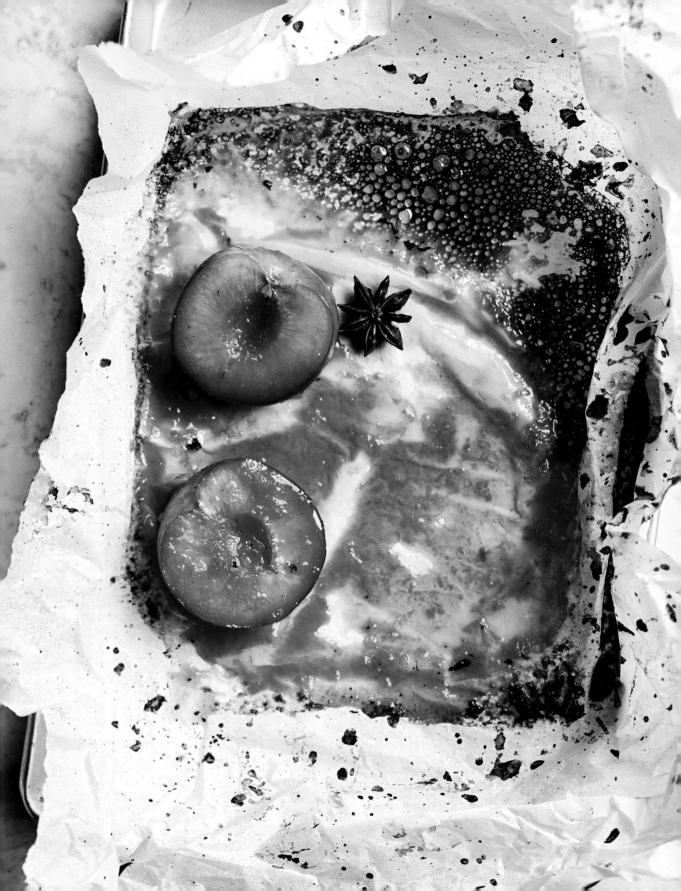

# Index

Note: page numbers in **bold** refer to illustrations.

# About the Authors

In 2015, three friends — Myles, Giles and Rob — were on a fishing boat in Devon, landing a catch so fresh that the locals queued up to get their hands on it. They had an idea: what if everyone in the UK had access to brilliant local produce? A few months later, Mindful Chef was born, with a mission to make healthy eating easy.

Mindful Chef creates recipe boxes packed with fresh, nutritionally balanced meals to cook at home. The food is so good, it's the UK's highest-rated recipe box company on Trustpilot.

Each week customers can choose from 20 recipes, as well as take their pick from a Ready to Go range full of nutritious smoothies and gut-happy breakfasts, lunches, dinners, snacks and desserts.

The recipes contain no refined carbs or sugars, and no dairy or gluten, to help you feel better. Ingredients are sourced from suppliers that adhere to strict environmental and welfare criteria: Mindful Chef boxes contain only 100% British grass-fed meat, free-range chicken and eggs, sustainably sourced fish, and UK fruit and veg comes from LEAF marque growers. The range also includes a selection of low-carbon options to help customers make kinder choices for the planet.

Mindful Chef has been certified as a B Corp since 2018 and is ranked in the top 3% of food and drinks B Corps globally. In 2017 it partnered with the charity One Feeds Two, so that for every meal purchased the company donates a school meal to a child living in poverty. To date it has donated over 16 million school meals. In 2022 it became the first recipe box company to implement a Regenerative Farming programme within its own supply chain, helping grow more good things for everyone.

mindfulchef.com

 @mindfulchefuk

 @mindfulchefuk

 /MindfulChef

# Acknowledgements

It has been six years since we wrote our first book *Eat Well, Live Better* and what a rollercoaster ride it has been. It is never easy growing a business, let alone a food business during a global pandemic, cost of living crisis and a recession. The time felt right to share and highlight all of the great things our company has achieved over those years.

To that end our biggest thank you must go to the people who make Mindful Chef so special – our team. We have always tried to surround ourselves with smart, caring, talented individuals who embody the Mindful Chef values and make coming to work so much more fun. Your passion and belief in delivering Mindful Chef's mission and making healthy eating easy for as many people as possible is what drives us to be better every single day.

A special mention must go to Jesse and JC for pulling together the amazing recipes in this book. To Richard and Emma for their help on the design and words written throughout. Thank you.

Thank you to Ben, Jess and the rest of the team at Penguin Random House for persuading us the time was right to release another book. Your unwavering support of Mindful Chef since the beginning has made the process ever more enjoyable.

To the wonderful team that brought our recipes to life: Steve, Ellie, George and Hannah, you should all be incredibly proud of your work – the food photography is amazing. Nicky, your design and artworking has been brilliant and you've really helped show off Mindful Chef in the best way possible. Imogen, thank you for steering the ship – we would not have been able to create such a beautiful and important book without your help.

To our families and friends for always supporting and believing in us from the very beginning. You are the people who really see what's going on everyday and help keep us going when times are tough. Thank you!

Finally, to our community and customers, to whom we owe a great deal of gratitude for your support and belief in our little idea. What started as three friends selling just three recipes each week has grown into something far, far bigger than we could ever have imagined. We have now delivered over 23 million recipes to more than 340,000 people. Thank you for believing in us and joining us on our mission to make healthy eating easy.

10 9 8 7 6 5 4 3 2 1

Century
20 Vauxhall Bridge Road
London SW1V 2SA

Century is part of the Penguin Random House group of companies whose addresses can be found at global.penguinrandomhouse.com.

Penguin
Random House
UK

First published by Century in 2023

www.penguin.co.uk

A CIP catalogue record for this book is available from the British Library.

ISBN 978 1 780 89670 0

Printed and bound in Italy by L.E.G.O. S.p.A

The authorised representative in the EEA is Penguin Random House Ireland, Morrison Chambers, 32 Nassau Street, Dublin D02 YH68.

www.greenpenguin.co.uk

Penguin Random House is committed to a sustainable future for our business, our readers and our planet. This book is made from Forest Stewardship Council® certified paper.

Creative Direction: Mindful Chef
Design: Nicky Barneby
Editor: Imogen Fortes
Recipe photography: Steven Joyce
Food styling: Ellie Mulligan
Food styling assistant: George Stocks
Prop styling: Hannah Wilkinson